THE 1868
ST. BERNARD PARISH
MASSACRE

THE 1868
ST. BERNARD PARISH
MASSACRE

Blood in the Cane Fields

C. DIER

THE
History
PRESS

Published by The History Press
Charleston, SC
www.historypress.net

First published 2017

Manufactured in the United States

ISBN 9781625858559

Library of Congress Control Number: 2017945028

Dedicated to
Lynne and Keith Dier, my parents, and
Conchetta Barranco Hausse, my late grandmother.

CONTENTS

ACKNOWLEDGEMENTS

To help highlight the history prior to the massacre, the massacre itself and how it shaped St. Bernard Parish, I am indebted to others for their assistance. William deMarigny Hyland, the current St. Bernard Parish historian, assisted with painting the events and the intricate history of the parish prior to 1868 in an accurate light. Jerry Estopinal, a prominent member of the Los Isleños Heritage and Cultural Society, also provided grave insight in this excursion. I would like to thank countless friends and family who assisted me throughout the process. Most importantly, I would like to extend an appreciation of gratitude to my mother, Lynne Dier, who instilled in me a burning passion for local history and advised me throughout this arduous process. She taught history in St. Bernard Parish for forty years before her retirement. I remain her student.

INTRODUCTION

On a cool October morning in 1868, Louis Wilson, a recently emancipated freedman, put on his finest clothes, hopped on his employer's horse and headed to the St. Bernard Parish Courthouse. He was a witness in an ongoing case. Wilson heard word "from town that the white people were going to come out and kill all the colored people" who were Republicans or "believed in the Union." Racial tensions were high over the upcoming presidential election. He had witnessed some freedmen being shot the night prior but assumed the worst was over.[1]

On his return from the courthouse, a group of white men led by Warren Check coerced Louis to dismount his horse, struck him in the jaw with a gun and tossed him into a wagon with other captive freedmen and Dr. Moses Lindley Lee, a wealthy white Republican from New York. The capturers transported the victims to Florey's, a local coffeehouse temporarily converted into a makeshift prison. They spoke of murdering Dr. Lee, but Wilson convinced them in Spanish and French that he was only there to make peace, not threaten others. Although Wilson was illiterate, he spoke English, French and Spanish, a feat that saved Dr. Lee's life.

The bandits delayed murdering Dr. Lee, but Wilson and other freedmen were not as fortunate. A few men dragged the freedmen onto the side of the road and, with little hesitation, shot them. Wilson survived, but the others died instantly. It was a brutal execution. Wilson, with a bullet lodged in his leg, managed to crawl into the nearby brush. One of the executioners approached him and shot him in the shoulder.

The perpetrators left Wilson for dead. He hid in the cane fields for three days until he felt safe to return home.

We do not know much about Wilson, but we do know these details from his testimony and concurring testimonies provided within a month of the ordeal. After giving testimony of his ordeal, he remarked, "This is such a cold bad place I am afraid I will die here. I want to be taken to a hospital."[2]

His story and similar others surrounding the course of events in St. Bernard Parish in 1868 have faded from memory. At the time of government investigations, the ordeal was frequently dubbed the "St. Bernard Riot," but there is no evidence of riot, only evidence of a massacre systemically orchestrated against the freedpeople of St. Bernard Parish. A riot presumes spontaneity or that similarly matched sides chaotically exchanged blows. Almost all freedpeople killed were unarmed. Considering this was a calculated event with all the characteristics of a massacre, it is labeled as a massacre in this book as opposed to a riot.

At least one investigation does label the events as a massacre. The Louisiana General Assembly (a common name for the Louisiana state legislature, which derives its origins from the French *Assemblée générale*) does not acknowledge the killings as riotous. According to the report, "The charge of 'negro riots' was hypocritical; it was intended solely to arouse the passions of the base and turbulent, so as to make them ready instruments of designing political leaders."[3]

I ORIGINALLY FOUND this story combing through the history of St. Bernard Parish as I taught eighth grade Louisiana history at St. Bernard Middle School, located in the region where the massacre occurred. St. Bernard Parish is directly adjacent to New Orleans on the same side of the river, the east bank. I searched local stories to help my students relate to the content and ignite interest. I was immediately captivated once I stumbled across this tragic and fascinating ordeal. I grew up in St. Bernard Parish, where these events occurred, and lived here almost my entire life. More importantly, I teach the descendants of many people mentioned in this work. I continue to have classes where students carry the last names of the victims and perpetrators.

In order to help comprehend the events leading up to the massacre, it is imperative to understand the multifaceted history of St. Bernard Parish prior to 1868. Establishing historic context is vital to more accurately comprehend an event or society. Much of the history regarding these

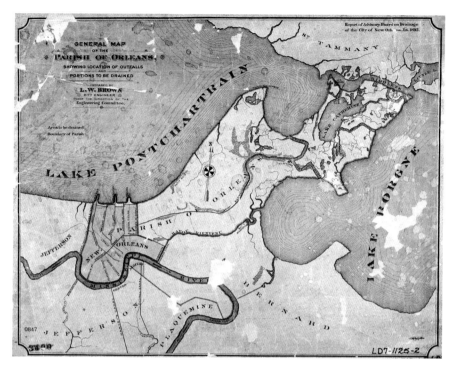

An 1895 map showing St. Bernard Parish in relation to New Orleans, Lake Pontchartrain, Lake Borgne and the Mississippi River. *Courtesy of the Historic New Orleans Collection.*

regions is focused on wealthy elites, typically plantation owners, bureaucrats or aristocrats who dictated important policy and economic decisions. Prior to the massacre, the two largest ethnic groups of St. Bernard were the Isleños, descendants of the Canary Islands, and Africans and their descendants, the majority of whom were locked in bondage until the Civil War. These two impoverished groups were at the forefront of the calamity.

To capture the story and the course of events before and after, I divided the chapters into chronological order. The first chapter, "Colonization," details the earliest groups who settled in the region and the early arrivals of Africans. It encompasses the arrival of the Isleños under Spanish rule. It also details the significant impact of the Louisiana Purchase and the Battle of New Orleans on the inhabitants of St. Bernard Parish. "Antebellum" is the title of the second chapter. The first section of the chapter covers St. Bernard Parish during the height of slavery and its role as the United States mobilized for war. The second section covers the Union invasion, subsequent occupation and its impact on the people of St. Bernard Parish, notably the emancipation of thousands of enslaved people, all of which had a profound impact on the buildup of the massacre itself.

The next four chapters focus specifically on the convoluted events surrounding the massacre. Chapter seven, "Deconstruction," discusses the ending of the massacre, its immediate impact on the region and its role in crippling Reconstruction efforts. Furthermore, it focuses on those who came to power after the death of Reconstruction and its effect on St. Bernard Parish. It highlights episodes of lynching and other atrocities employed to intimidate African Americans and preserve white dominance. Lastly, chapter eight, "Recollection," discusses St. Bernard Parish as it transitioned into the twentieth century and set the stage to morph into its current character as the events of 1868 faded from collective memory.

This saga is hardly mentioned throughout history. Perhaps the most documented account of this story is from a report, "The St. Bernard Riot, 1868," written by First Lieutenant Jesse Matlock Lee. Lieutenant Lee was born in Indiana, joined the Union army at the outbreak of the Civil War and was later tasked to investigate riots and disturbances throughout Louisiana during Reconstruction. At the age of twenty-six, he visited St. Bernard Parish for a day, interviewed at least eleven victims and hastily wrote a report to his superiors. Beyond Lieutenant Lee's report, only a handful of books concerning Reconstruction violence in Louisiana give it slight attention. There are no dissertations or articles in historical journals. There are no historical markers to remember it or to memorialize the black victims. Much, if not all, of the story has been lost through oral tradition. Nonetheless, the stories of Louis Wilson and others who faced such brutality need to be told.

Chapter 1

COLONIZATION

They asked him who his comrades were;
Poor St. Malo said not a word!
The judge his sentence read to him,
And then they raised the gallows-tree.
They drew the horse—the cart moved off—
And left St. Malo hanging there.
The sun was up an hour high
When on the Levee he was hung;
They left his body swinging there,
For carrion crows to feed upon.
—"The Dirge of San Malo" [4]

I t was a scorching summer day in 1784 as New Orleanians of various social classes poured into Plaza de Armas (today Jackson Square) in the French Quarter to see what was at that time considered a grand spectacle: the lynching of three black men for murdering whites. No clergy administrated their final confessions, an atypical act for even the harshest of criminals; instead, they opted to watch from their balcony overlooking the plaza. The main fugitive, Juan San Malo, unsuccessfully attempted to exonerate his two companions from the gallows. The floor of the gallows soon gave way, and three bodies dangled.[5]

In the late eighteenth century in Spanish Louisiana, Juan San Malo and his group of maroons roamed the marshes surrounding New Orleans. The word "maroon" derives from the Spanish word *cimarrón*, which roughly translates to "fugitive" or "runaway." San Malo was one of Louisiana's fiercest and most notable maroons. Little is known about his upbringing. Prior to mutinying, he belonged to Karl Friedrich D'Arensbourg, a Swiss-born colonial official with a plantation along the German Coast, a region along the Mississippi River above New Orleans. After Malo's escape, he utilized his carpentry skills to produce furniture to accumulate weapons and gunpowder. His alarming success gained him loyal supporters throughout the maroon community. He established his main camp in Bas du Fleuve, located in modern-day St. Bernard Parish along the banks of Lake Borgne. Bas du Fleuve and surrounding regions were notorious for *marronage*. The majority of maroons from the area hailed from St. Bernard Parish, considering its geographical features and proximity to New Orleans paved the way for large plantations.[6]

The first ships carrying enslaved Africans arrived in New Orleans in 1719, and by as early as 1723, maps depict large plantations fronting the Mississippi River within the modern-day borders of St. Bernard Parish. The majority of the earliest slave ships that arrived in French Louisiana were from Senegambia, modern-day Senegal and Gambia. The Senegambians were from a sophisticated culture skilled at ironworking, farming and various other tasks. They successfully cultivated indigo, which grew wild in both Senegal and Louisiana. It became a lucrative cash crop in early Louisiana. Some Africans fled from brutal slave conditions to the swampy environment surrounding the plantations that provided an elusive escape. Bas du Fleuve and similar places provided San Malo and other maroons a plentiful source of runaways.[7]

Maroons living in Bas du Fleuve started out as raiders plundering to survive. However, their modus operandi shifted as they became more organized under San Malo's leadership. According to Gwendolyn Midlo Hall in *Africans in Colonial Louisiana: The Development of Afro-Creole Culture in the Eighteenth Century*:

> *Although some of the maroons continued to raid plantations and kill cattle, there was a move toward production and trade for economic survival. They cultivated corn, squash, and rice and gathered and ground herbs for food. They made baskets, sifters, and other articles woven from willow and reeds. They carved indigo vats and troughs from cypress wood. And…they gathered berries, dwarf palmetto roots, and sassafras, trapped birds, hunted and fished, and went to New Orleans to trade and to gamble. Although*

Left: A 1723 map of the New Orleans area depicting property owners along the Mississippi River. *Courtesy of Newberry Library, Chicago.*

Below: A 1707 French map depicting Senegambia along coastal West Africa. *Courtesy of the Library of Congress.*

the maroons were denounced as brigands and murderers, their violence was almost entirely defensive. The danger they posed to the colony was more profound. They surrounded the plantations. Slaves remaining with their masters were in constant contact with them.[8]

San Malo's name possibly derives from the slave-trading port of Saint-Malo in northwestern France, but it is uncertain. The named sounded like "Saint Evil" in Spanish. Stories of him reverberated throughout Spanish Louisiana and terrified the Creole elite and wealthy slave owners. (The term "Creole" refers to people descended from early colonial settlers, usually of French, Spanish and/or African origins.) San Malo was known for his harsh tactics at remaining a free person. According to folklore, he murdered his wife for desiring to return to her owner because she feared being caught. Although San Malo and his group were typically defensive, they sometimes attacked people transporting slaves to emancipate others and potentially enlarge their coalition. According to another legend, he stabbed a tree near his encampment and claimed, "*Malheur au blanc qui passera ces borners*" ["Woe to the white who would pass this boundary"]. He also kept dangerous company. One of his loyal lieutenants was nicknamed "Knight of the Axe" because of his choice of weapon used to brutally split open the head of an American captor who made the unfortunate mistake of venturing his way.[9]

The Spanish colonial government repeatedly ordered unsuccessful raids to capture the fugitive maroon San Malo. He and his maroons, usually comprising over one hundred armed men, would rather die than succumb to the brutality of slavery. The Spanish elite considered the maroon a threat that needed to be immediately eradicated. In 1794, they mounted a surprise invasion consisting of regular troops, militiamen, hunters and others who desired San Malo dead. Guided by a tip from San Malo's captured companions, they plunged into the marshes with pirogues, flat-bottomed boats commonly used in shallow waters, full of heavily armed men. They attacked the camp and captured San Malo with sixteen other men.[10]

An injured San Malo pleaded to be finished off, but his captors wanted glory for subduing the evasive maroon. According to Gilbert C. Din in *Spaniards, Planters, and Slaves*, "Word of San Malo's apprehension spread quickly, and many inhabitants lined the Mississippi to cheer the boats as they passed. About June 10, onlookers at New Orleans crowded the levee and the houses facing the river to see the pirogues bringing the captives."

San Malo was paraded around New Orleans as citizens jeered and hurled insults. During his trial, he confessed to the murder of whites. After a guilty verdict, San Malo was lynched in Plaza de Armas. Other maroons faced endless flogging, brandings of the letter "*M*" for maroon, shackling and other forms of torture. Malo's new wife, Cecilia, was sentenced to execution but was spared because she was pregnant.[11]

San Malo's ability to stand up to brute oppression was recognized among the local slave community. He continued to live as a legend throughout the region for well over a century following his death. His gallantry was the subject of a popular Creole song in St. Bernard Parish, "The Dirge of San Malo," and is documented in George Washington Cable's 1886 work, *Creole Slave Songs*. According to Lawrence Powell in *The Accidental City*, the song "portrayed the maroon chieftain as biting his tongue when asked to implicate his comrades, and which could still be heard in St. Bernard Parish long after Emancipation, was not just a song of lament but a testament to the slaves' defiance."[12]

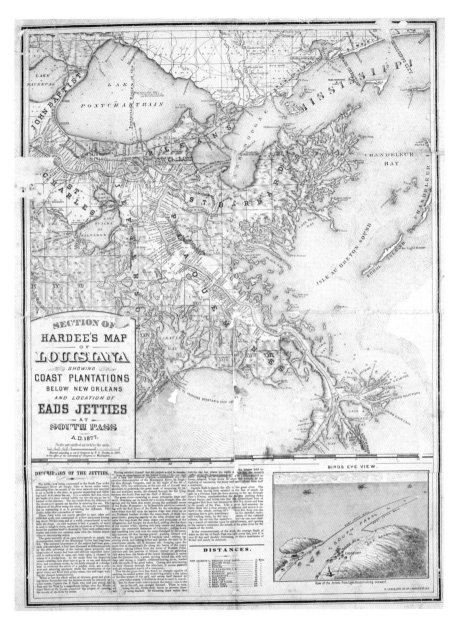

An 1877 map of the New Orleans area specifying plantations along the Mississippi River. St. Bernard Parish is southeast of New Orleans. *Courtesy of the Historic New Orleans Collection.*

An illustration in *Harper's Weekly* depicting various dwellings in Saint Malo, 1883. *Courtesy of the Library of Congress.*

His legacy helped inspire the failed German Coast Uprising along the Mississippi River in 1811, the largest slave insurrection in United States history. San Malo did more than inspire hope for a life of freedom for the enslaved. Sometime between the 1820s and 1830s, a Spanish ship leaving the Spanish East Indies, present-day Philippines, docked at New Orleans. A group of Filipinos seized the opportunity to abandon ship. These Filipinos, skilled and adept at life on the water, sought refuge on the shores of Lake Borgne, in modern-day St. Bernard Parish, away from the hustle and bustle of one of the largest ports in the Americas. They named their newfound settlement Saint Malo after hearing stories of the legend. It was the first Filipino settlement in the United States. Saint Malo existed in almost complete isolation as a self-sufficient village for well over a century until a hurricane in 1915 obliterated the community.[13]

COMMUNITIES WITH MAROONS like San Malo helped shape the complex and diverse region where local Native American, German, French and Spanish inhabitants all lived in proximity. The Isleños, Spanish for islanders, were another early ethnic group of St. Bernard Parish. From 1778 to 1783, the Isleños emigrated from the Canary Islands, a Spanish mountainous archipelago in the Atlantic Ocean about sixty-two miles west of Morocco. Spain colonized the islands and almost entirely wiped out the resistant native Guanche population. In 1492, Christopher Columbus stopped on one of the islands, La Gomera, on his first voyage to the Americas to repair his ships and restock.

The events leading up to the arrival of the Isleños are complex. The French and Indian War broke out between France and Great Britain in 1754. Louisiana was a colony of France until 1762, when France ceded Louisiana to Spain in exchange for assistance against the British. At first, Spain considered the territory a liability. However, from a military perspective, Spain agreed to the treaty to prevent Great Britain from obtaining and posing a threat to the Spanish territories of Texas and Mexico.[14]

Spain immediately conducted a census on communities throughout Spanish Louisiana. Bas du Fleuve had a population of over two thousand, the majority of whom were slaves and maroons. Whites, Native Americans and indentured servants also present. The Spanish government quickly became aware of the economy of the maroons, especially in terms of their mastery with cutting and squaring cypress logs.[15]

The transfer of Louisiana to Spain did not stop the influx of francophone immigrants to the colony, especially after the Acadians— referred to today as Cajuns—migrated after their expulsion from Canada by the British. Spain needed to populate the region for a variety of purposes: to combat the existing and growing francophone culture, for basic protection against the English and in case the newly founded United States decided to expand. The impoverished and illiterate population of the Canary Islands provided an illustrious solution. The Spanish Crown

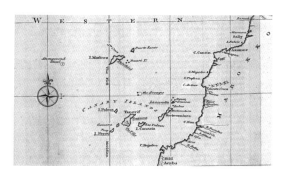

A 1745 map of the Canary Islands off the coast of Morocco. *Courtesy of the New York Public Library.*

21

An oil painting of Bernardo de Gálvez by Mariano Salvador Maella Pérez, circa 1783. Gálvez was the fifth Spanish governor of Louisiana and oversaw the arrival of the Isleños. St. Bernard Parish received its name from him. *Mariano Salvador Maella, courtesy Wikimedia Commons.*

ordered seven hundred Canary Islanders to settle Louisiana. Some Canary Islanders initially resisted, but to no avail.[16]

Starting in 1778, hundreds of Isleños embarked toward the Spanish colonies either by coercion, recruitment or a hope for a better life. The Spanish government attempted to establish four key settlements in various areas around New Orleans, the most prominent and successful being in lower St. Bernard Parish. Spanish documents refer to the region as *Nueva Galvez*, *Concepcion* and *St. Bernard*, the latter of which evidently emerged as the primary name.[17]

Bernardo de Gálvez, the Spanish governor of Louisiana from 1777 to 1785, oversaw the arrival of the Isleños to Louisiana. Gálvez played a prominent role in both Spanish and United States history. He assisted the thirteen colonies during the American Revolution by smuggling weapons and supplies to the rebels, protecting French colonies in the Gulf of Mexico and conquering British Florida for the Spanish Crown. St. Bernard Parish is named after his patron saint, Saint Bernard of Clairvaux, following an archaic tradition customary with Catholic monarchies.[18]

Gálvez and French Creole Pierre DeMarigny, the St. Bernard Parish commandant, chose *Terre-aux-Boeufs*, "land of cattle," located in lower St. Bernard Parish, for the Isleños settlement. The reasons are probably twofold. First, the upper part of what is now St. Bernard Parish was already inhabited by profitable plantations settled by the French. Second, a settlement there could provide a crucial buffer and allow the Isleños to help defend New Orleans in case of an attack from that direction.[19]

Life in the flat Louisiana swamps was much different than the volcanic Canary Islands. Louisiana provided much different challenges: bugs, harsher climate, snakes, floods and one of the most problematic of all obstacles, hurricanes. Repeated floods and hurricanes in 1779 and 1780 forced the majority of the Isleños at Barataria to relocate. With permission from DeMarigny, they settled in Terre-aux-Boeufs with their Isleños counterparts. St. Bernard had three separate thriving Isleños communities, with the Barataria Isleños establishing the fourth.[20]

Upon arrival, the Isleños in St. Bernard Parish had their food rationed and received land grants, housing and other sources of welfare from the Spanish government. They became skilled fishermen who caught shrimp, oysters, crawfish, alligators, crabs, various fish and whatever else the water provided. They raised animals and grew agriculture. In 1782, DeMarigny wrote to Spanish administrators that the Isleños settlements in Terre-aux-Boeufs were completely self-sufficient.[21]

The Isleños migration ended in 1783 as the last three ships departed Cuba for St. Bernard Parish. However, migration from Spanish settlers did not cease. The parish was opened by Spanish officials to ex-military personnel who did not want to return to Spain. St. Bernard Parish also provided refuge for discharged Spanish soldiers and sailors. Some Isleños from Terre-aux-Boeufs assisted Gálvez's quests in the American Revolution (the exact numbers are unknown). This might have provided a source for some veterans looking for Spanish settlements in the region.[22]

In 1786, Terre-aux-Boeufs saw the arrival of Acadians. Intermarriage between the two groups was common, and it is still common among their descendants. The Acadians and Isleños shared the same religion, Catholicism, despite many linguistic and cultural differences between them. In 1787, construction began on the St. Bernard Church and the St. Bernard Cemetery. In 1791, the area was granted a tavern.[23]

A renovated house depicting early Isleños settlements at the Los Isleños Heritage and Multi-Cultural Museum. *Author's collection.*

Renovated homes and agricultural tools at the Los Isleños Heritage and Multi-Cultural Museum. *Author's collection.*

Left: The entrance sign to the St. Bernard Cemetery. *Author's collection.*

Middle: The entrance to the St. Bernard Cemetery. *Courtesy of Rhett Pritchard.*

Bottom: St. Bernard Catholic Church. *Author's collection.*

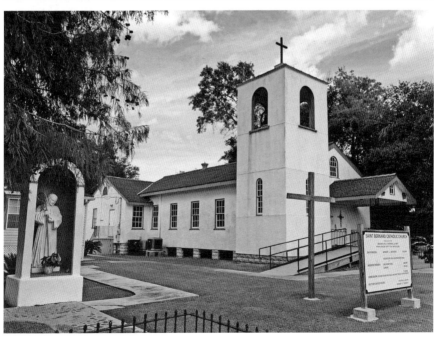

In 1792, a groundbreaking achievement in St. Bernard Parish transformed the parish and the regional economy. Don Antonio Mendez, a Spanish officer living in Terre-aux-Boeufs, successfully granulated sugar. Mendez sold seed cane to Etienne de Boré, whose plantation stood where Audubon Park in the Uptown neighborhood of New Orleans is currently located. De Boré commercialized the industry. St. Bernard Parish morphed into a sugar-producing powerhouse that would boost its economy and significantly alter the demographics of the parish.[24]

THE EARLY DEMANDS for cash crops led to an extension of slavery within the region. A census from the Spanish colonial government in the mid-1790s showed sixty-one enslaved persons in St. Bernard Parish, although this was probably an underestimate, as the purpose of the census was to collect a tax on slaves. This census excludes many of the plantations fronting the Mississippi River because those plantations were not located historically within the borders of St. Bernard Parish during the colonial era. None of the impoverished Isleños communities owned slaves. Race relations between the Isleños and the enslaved were consistently stable. Documents show many Isleños sold patches of land to free people of color and lived in proximity without provocation. Some Isleños left property and other possessions to black acquaintances in their wills.[25]

This semblance of camaraderie between ethnicities was not as common with marooning communities. The majority of runaway slaves were often compelled to steal in order to survive in a state of existence considered illegal. They had not been a major cause of concern since the lynching of Juan San Malo; however, they again became an issue at the turn of the century as they marauded for food and resources. In 1799, French Creole slave owners in what is now considered St. Bernard Parish complained to the governor about excessive theft of property and animals. The maroons, outcast by society, also stole property from Isleños farmers. The evil institution of slavery forced those seeking freedom into exile and, at times, starvation. This inevitably led to conflict between impoverished groups competing for resources. This created additional hardship for the struggling Isleños settlements. The Spanish government put bounties on maroons, mostly to protect the property of slave owners, but it had little, if any, impact.[26]

The land now considered St. Bernard Parish was vastly eclectic as it entered the nineteenth century. French Creoles owned plantations in the upper part of the region with hundreds of enslaved people who toiled the land. Armed maroons roamed around Lake Borgne and established Bas du Fleuve and other makeshift communities. Filipinos thrived in their own isolated community, Saint Malo. Hundreds of Isleños and other Spaniards lived self-sufficiently and intermarried with Acadians in Terre-aux-Boeufs. Heavy trade probably existed between these early ethnic groups. In the first two decades of the nineteenth century, the region would be significantly altered by two lasting events: the Louisiana Purchase and the Battle of New Orleans.

In 1800, Spain signed the Treaty of San Ildefonso and returned Louisiana to France as Napoleon Bonaparte desired the establishment of an empire in the French colony. Napoleon's ambitions were thwarted due to various factors, most notably a successful slave revolution led by Toussaint L'Ouverture that resulted in a loss of Saint-Domingue, present-day Haiti. Haiti became the second independent republic in the Americas. The loss of a profitable colony combined with a need to fund its militaristic endeavors in Europe prompted France to sell its territory to the United States.

Thomas Jefferson sent Robert Livingston to New Orleans in an attempt to purchase the city to control an important entrance to the interior of North America. Since Napoleon was desperate for finances, he sold the entire Louisiana territory to the United States for a mere $15 million, less than three cents an acre. The Louisiana Purchase doubled the size of the United States and remains the largest real estate transaction in history. Spain protested the transfer because France agreed not to sell the land to a third party in the Treaty of San Ildefonso, but Spain was in no position to contest Napoleon. St. Bernard Parish thus fell under American rule.

Reactions to the transaction were probably heavily mixed in St. Bernard Parish. It is uncertain how the Isleños or those enslaved reacted to the sale. However, it is certain how the Americans reacted to the Isleños. Governor William C.C. Claiborne was the first American governor of Louisiana. He spoke no Spanish or French, a problem for a state where only one-sixth of the population spoke English at the time and a problem for St. Bernard Parish, where almost all inhabitants spoke Spanish, French or various African languages. Claiborne sent Dr. John Watkins to assess the settlements in St. Bernard Parish. According to Gilbert C. Din in his book *The Canary Islanders of Louisiana*, Dr. Watkins characterized "the inhabitants as humble, poor, indolent, and ignorant" simpletons who "idolize" their priests. At the time of transaction, roughly eight hundred people lived in the parish.[27]

THE NEW REPUBLIC faced many challenges shortly after the Louisiana Purchase. Peace between the United States and Great Britain was short-lived. A motive for new territory coupled with resentment toward Great Britain prompted President James Madison to declare a war that would forever change St. Bernard Parish. The War of 1812 began miserably for the young United States. As the British burned Washington, D.C., to rubble, the country was again left to defend itself against one of the mightiest empires in the world. Great Britain planned three invasions of the United States. Capturing New Orleans was the goal of the third invasion. Major General Andrew Jackson was tasked to defend the city.

Jackson's army marched to New Orleans to meet the formidable British force, which included Native Americans and maroons from Spanish Florida, led by the famed Lieutenant General Sir Edward Michael Pakenham, brother-in-law of the Duke of Wellington. Both armies were unaware that representatives from their respective countries had already signed the Treaty of Ghent, which declared the war over. However, the British capture of New Orleans would have been an attractive bargaining chip as both countries ratified the treaty.[28]

Both Great Britain and the United States sought the recruitment of a well-armed contingent of pirates from Barataria Bay led by Jean Lafitte. Lafitte's settlement was not far from the original Isleños community that attempted to settle before migrating to St. Bernard Parish. The factors that made permanent settlement difficult are the same factors that provided Lafitte with the necessary elusiveness to run his illegal operations. His empire consisted of hundreds of rogue men with an intimate knowledge of the waterways. These men looted and smuggled so excessively that Governor Claiborne offered a bounty of $500 for Lafitte's head; Lafitte counteroffered a $5,000 bounty for Claiborne's head.[29]

The British offered Lafitte a position in the Royal Navy and $30,000 and promised to protect his land and assets. The Americans offered to release captured pirates and amnesty for past crimes. Lafitte pledged his allegiance to the Americans. Jackson reluctantly accepted the pirates as allies after he unintentionally met Lafitte in the French Quarter.[30]

Jackson's arrival was bittersweet. New Orleanians were skeptical but needed protection. Jackson was also skeptical of a city inhabited by people he hardly considered Americans. He declared martial law in the city and the surrounding areas, including St. Bernard Parish. A judge and a lawyer who opposed the draconian measure were immediately detained.[31]

Anglo-Americans who lived in New Orleans welcomed Jackson. He managed to arouse Creole support because of their mutual hatred of the British. He also accepted a large battalion of local free men of color. He placed confidence in their abilities and loyalties and called them "brave fellow citizens." Jackson, a slave owner himself, was no friend to people of color, but he needed the support.[32]

THE ROYAL NAVY entered Lake Borgne in St. Bernard Parish in late December 1814, not far from the town of Saint Malo, and quickly overwhelmed American gunboats in the Battle of Lake Borgne. The loss allowed the British to safely land in Bayou Bienvenue in St. Bernard Parish. The British visited a small fishermen's village to find scouts to help survey the land to decipher how to best approach New Orleans. A few village residents of Spanish and Portuguese origin provided pirogues, gave reconnaissance information and served as guides for the British, perhaps not by choice. The British maneuvered to a sugar cane plantation in Chalmette owned by Major General Jacques Villeré, a prominent figure throughout Louisiana politics and then commander of the Louisiana State Militia. His home was a mere nine miles downriver from the city.[33]

The British quickly attacked Villeré's plantation, freed all fifty-two slaves and used it as their headquarters. Jacques Villeré's son, Gabriel Villeré, escaped through a window as British soldiers tried to shoot him. British pursuit was hopeless once Villeré retreated to the swamps. He went to another plantation in Chalmette owned by Colonel Pierre Denis de La Ronde. Villeré and de La Ronde boarded a boat and quickly paddled up the Mississippi River to the French Quarter to notify Jackson of the British location.[34]

Meanwhile, the British marched about a mile closer to an unprepared New Orleans. However, General John Keane decided to halt to wait

Battle of Lake Borgne. *Courtesy of Rhett Pritchard.*

Wilson Chinn wearing a torture instrument used to keep potential runaways from resting their heads. *Private collection, courtesy of William L. Schaeffer.*

for reinforcements. Keane set up camp and ignored the pleas of lower-ranking officials to continue marching. The British felt overly confident about their position. One officer remarked that he was excited to spend "carnival" in New Orleans.[35]

Many British troops marched into Terre-aux-Boeufs and stole approximately forty horses and supplies from the Isleños. The Isleños were never compensated for their losses. The British also hired or freed slaves, mainly to disrupt the local economy. Slave owners of St. Bernard Parish met with British officers to regain what they considered property but only received one of the some three hundred who deserted.[36]

At the British camp, dozens of enslaved persons from nearby plantations sought refuge and protection. They were put to work in strenuous conditions to assist the British in their preparations. The British soldiers documented their conditions. One runaway in particular approached an officer and asked in French if the officer could remove his collar of spikes that had been placed on him as punishment for having intentions of fleeing. The spikes hindered the man's ability to lie down to sleep or rest. It was a glimpse of the brutality faced at the hands of planters in the area. The officer, impressed with the maroon's ability to speak French, Spanish and "a little English," made a derisive comment regarding America as the "land of liberty" before he ordered the blacksmith to remove the collar.[37]

The British found such treatment a contradiction to the principles pledged by the United States. However, in order to win over the local population against the Americans, the invading army ensured that slavery would not be abolished under British occupation. They printed signs in French and Spanish and plastered them to plantation fences: "Louisianians! Remain quiet in your houses; your slaves shall be preserved to you, and your property respected. We make war only against Americans."[38]

IN JACKSON'S HEADQUARTERS, Villeré's rushed French was translated to English. Once Jackson realized the severity of the situation, he rose out of his chair and yelled, "By the Eternal, they shall not sleep on our soil!" The U.S. Army, free men of color, Choctaw Indians, militias from around the South, local French Creoles and Isleños from St. Bernard Parish marched in unison to meet the British. The diverse group demonstrated a unique solidarity as the British threatened their home and livelihood.[39]

Jackson utilized the Macarty Plantation in Chalmette as his headquarters after launching a few surprise skirmishes on British outposts. Both sides exchanged artillery blows as they prepared for inevitable battle. On the morning of January 8, 1815, a contingent of British troops crossed the Mississippi River to attack from the west bank. The British misjudged the intensity of the river and landed farther south than anticipated. The main British forces attacked Jackson's main lines but were continually repulsed. The British retreated after multiple failed waves of attack. Approximately 285 British soldiers died, while only 13 American soldiers were killed. The Battle of New Orleans was a strategic blunder for the British.

One New Orleans merchant wrote that "the field of slaughter was covered with bodies of British soldiers, lying either dead or wounded. I call it the field of slaughter; for it really was slaughter." Many women of color assisted the wounded. One British officer wrote, "Several women of colour offered their services, and were employed in tending them, without any compensation but the pleasure of relieving suffering humanity."[40]

General Pakenham was mortally wounded during the mayhem. His heart and other organs were cut out and buried under pecan trees. His body was embalmed in a barrel of rum for conservation and returned home. One writer wittingly remarked that Pakenham was sent back in good spirits.[41]

The British withdrew from the region after a month of failed attempts at taking Fort St. Philip in Plaquemines Parish and failures elsewhere along the Gulf coast. The victory sent shockwaves throughout the country and birthed a renewed sense of nationalism. Many participants went on to more famous roles. Jacques Villeré, who commanded the Louisiana militia, was the first Creole governor of Louisiana and the only St. Bernardian to hold that office. Renato Beluche, a French Creole who lived on the Chalmette Plantation, was another local who participated in the battle. After the battle, he joined Simon Bolivar's revolutionary campaigns across South America. Andrew Jackson eventually became president.

Some of the enslaved ran in fear during the British invasion. Many were whipped upon return. Another popular French Creole song sung by African Americans well into the late nineteenth century highlighted a slave who decided to run during the battle:

Cannons align the Chalmette Battlefield where the Battle of New Orleans was fought. *Courtesy of Rhett Pritchard.*

The English muskets went bim! Bim!
Kentucky rifles went zim! Zim!
I said to myself, save your skin!
I scampered along the water's edge;
When I got back it was day break.
Mistress flew into a passion;
She had me whipped at the "four stakes,"
Because I didn't stay with master;
But the "four stakes" for me is better than
A musket shot from an Englishmen.[42]

The Battle of New Orleans had a profound impact on St. Bernard Parish. The immediate aftermath was one of utter destruction not seen until Hurricane Katrina in 2005. Many Isleños had to sell their land grants to sugar planters who consolidated the tracts into sugar estates. Other planters whose plantations were ruined from the battle or other skirmishes sold their properties and were financially ruined. Decades later, the victory against the British gave the parish a proud identity. It was an era when multiple ethnicities joined forces to tackle a common foe. A list of volunteers showed many Isleños fought with their new country. Chalmette received its namesake from one of the battleground plantations. Many streets in Chalmette, notably around Andrew Jackson Middle School, are named in honor of officers from both sides. A main thoroughfare is named after Jean Lafitte. However, one group might not have celebrated as loudly as the rest. Thousands remained enslaved on the plantations of St. Bernard Parish as the parish entered the antebellum era.

Chapter 2

ANTEBELLUM

And if you say, "Lawd a-mercy," de overseer whip you.
De old people, dey just set down and cry.
—Ceceil George, former slave

Many prominent figures visited St. Bernard Parish because of the Battle of New Orleans. In 1825, the Marquis de Lafayette, a renowned French military officer who fought in the American Revolution, arrived on the steamboat *Natchez* to thunderous applause at the Macarty Plantation during his triumphal tour of the United States. Harriet Martineau, an English social theorist and early feminist sociologist, wrote in 1838 about her visit to St. Bernard Parish in *Retrospect to Western Travel*. Martineau remarked on the aesthetics of the area: "With the Mississippi on the right hand, and on the left gardens of roses which bewildered the imagination. I really believed at the time that I saw more roses that morning than during the whole course of my life before." The battlefield itself garnered different feelings: "It was a deadly battlefield. It makes the spectator shudder to see the wide open space, the unsheltered level, over which the British soldiers were compelled to march to certain destruction." Martineau wrote heavily about slavery in other writings; however, despite visiting plantations, it was not a center of focus for her visit to St. Bernard Parish.[43]

The year 1838 saw another visitor to St. Bernard Parish, a writer from the New Orleans–based *Weekly Picayune*. The writer's article, "Some Interesting Glimpses of Louisiana a Century Ago," highlighted the Isleños and their customs in the years before the "overwhelming tide of improvement, innovation and all kinds of Americanism" completely eradicated their archaic way of life. The Isleños, to him, appeared relatively unchanged from colonial days. His article described how they lived off the land, mastered the art of training oxen and sold their goods in New Orleans markets. The Isleños' trips to the markets were family affairs. According to the author, planters came from other areas of Louisiana to learn how to properly train oxen from the Isleños. He described their homes as "rude" and claimed that the people were incredibly polite, shared their excesses, upheld societal virtues, respected their elders and were overall blissful. His New Orleans audience was intrigued by the nearby communities they hardly knew existed.[44]

There was an influx of American newcomers during the antebellum days to Terre-aux-Boeufs to establish plantations. Most purchased fertile land from the Isleños, pushing the Isleños geographically closer to African Americans. According to Gilbert Din in *The Canary Islanders of Louisiana*, the parish was shaped into three distinct regions around this time: upper St. Bernard, which was made up mainly of wealthy plantations; middle St. Bernard, which was primarily small farms in Terre-aux-Boeufs held by Isleños; and the lower parish, which consisted of Delacroix and nearby areas, where the Isleños lived in proximity to the water and were relatively secluded from the outside world.[45]

THE DEMOGRAPHIC MAKEUP of the parish remained relatively unaltered during the antebellum period until St. Bernard Parish received an influx of immigrants from Europe and former Spanish colonies. Most immigrants hailed from Spain, Ireland, France, Germany, Cuba and Mexico. Many had likely heard of the settlement while in New Orleans and were attracted to the area for its land and agricultural opportunities and its already sizeable population of Spanish speakers. The slight addition of Cubans and Mexicans contributed to the existing Hispanic character of the parish, but the census of 1850 shows that the influx of whites had a much larger impact on area demographics. As a result of the influx, Isleños now composed slightly less than 50 percent of the white population and were no longer the white majority. The loss of this majority, coupled with black male voter enfranchisement, played an essential role in the violence to come.[46]

The overwhelming majority of Isleños lived humble lives, with the notable exceptions of Estevan Nunez and Antonio Marrero. Nunez accrued some wealth as a sugar cane planter and became a slave owner. Marrero owned seventy-one slaves in 1850, and his property, which spanned over 1,500 acres, was valued at more than $100,000. Modern-day Marrero, a town with a population of approximately thirty-seven thousand on the west bank of the Mississippi River, is named after his cousin Louis. The majority of Isleños were far removed from the wealth acquired by Marrero and lived antiquated lifestyles that attracted the attention and fascination of those who visited the parish. In 1851, a visiting New England woman expressed her admiration in a letter to a friend: "There is a kind of fish caught here called a cat fish which nobody thinks fitting to eat but the Spaniards [Isleños] over the river, and there they sit with their dogs all day long in the sun, close to the water's edge, fishing and singing at their work. I love dearly to hear them; in the evening they build large fires along the bank for decoys, they look beautifully in the dark."[47]

As WITH MANY sugar cane parishes, the brutality of slavery dominated antebellum St. Bernard Parish. If a man was coerced to wear a spiked collar that forbade him to rest for the *mere thought* of leaving, one might imagine the lack of humanity with which punishment was meted out to those who acted on their fierce desire to escape the violence of the plantations. Victims who gave testimonies after the massacre of 1868 were likely enslaved prior to the Civil War, though their testimonies focused not on their experiences as enslaved people but on the events of the massacre itself. Perhaps the most detailed account of the slave experience in St. Bernard Parish comes from Ceceil George, who was interviewed by the Federal Writers' Project of the Works Progress Administration (WPA) in 1940. George was born in 1846 and was ninety-four years old at the time of the interview. Her account began with her upbringing in South Carolina until the day she was sold: "De missis and her daughter, dey kept de Big House and some of de slaves, but some of us had to go. Dey sold us like a gang of chickens, my family and plenty more. I remember well. We all cried [when we had] to leave de old country [South Carolina], but we had more tears dan dat to shed."[48]

George was sold to a wealthy plantation owner in lower St. Bernard Parish. George continued her narrative by describing the journey by steamship, which left South Carolina, curled around Florida and ventured up the Gulf of Mexico before arriving at her new quarters. She believed that her transporters had chosen to move slaves by sea not because it was an efficient means of travel but because it effectively undermined efforts to escape. "Dey made us go by de sea because den we can't go back," she noted. She continued describing her new quarters:

> *It was a big place, twenty houses in de quarters, all de houses packed wid people. O Lawd, I come up in hard times, slavery-times.*
>
> *Everybody worked, young and old. If you could only carry two or three sugar cane [stalks], you worked. No school, no church—you couldn't sing—and Saturday night dey always have a dance, but you worked. Sunday, Monday, it all de same. And if you say, "Lawd a-mercy," de overseer whip you. De old people, dey just set down and cry. It [was] like a heathern [sic] part of de country. You has to put your candle out early and shut yourself up, den get up while it's still dark and start to work.*
>
> *In de old country you never have a scratch. Dey never whips deir slaves—lock dem up, yes, but don't whip dem. Down here dey strip you down naked, and two men hold you down and whip you till de blood come. Cruel! O Lawd.*
>
> *So mind I tell you what I seed wid my own eyes. De people take sick and dey die, [but] dere ain't no coffin for dem. Dey take planks and nail dem together like a chicken coop.*[49]

She remarked about the "old clothes, one pair [of] shoes a year, no stockings, and in de winter sometimes you so cold." Thousands of slaves in St. Bernard Parish undoubtedly faced similarly horrific conditions. The 1860 census shows an enslaved population of 2,240, with 120 slaveholders, 14 of whom owned more than 50 slaves. The overall 1860 population of the parish, including enslaved people, stood at 4,076. Thus, more than half the population was locked in bondage, and despite being the majority, they possessed no opportunity for political or economic advancement.[50]

The phenomenon of a politically and economically hamstrung majority existed throughout all sugar cane–dominated parishes. In 1860, the white population of the sugar-producing parishes, excluding New Orleans, was 60,356, with the enslaved population totaling 88,439. Although the majority of whites in St. Bernard Parish and other sugar parishes were not slave owners, the entire white population benefited from the institution of forced labors, especially in terms of local politics due to white male suffrage.[51]

Before the Civil War, the presence of slavery in what is now the current borders of St. Bernard Parish spanned at least 138 years. As the demand for sugar increased, the parish transformed from a society with slaves to a slavery-dependent society. As such, the systemic brutality became ingrained within the fabric of the parish. The area's slave-operated sugar plantations were mainly owned by French Creoles and incoming opportunistic Americans, some of whom established their plantations on land purchased from Isleños. The Isleños during this period continued to live simply and, for the most part, kept to themselves.

The year 1861 was the last in which many wealthy plantation owners enjoyed undisrupted success in St. Bernard Parish. Throughout the nation, a battle waged over the divisive issue of slavery. Slavery remained deeply entrenched in the antebellum South, despite its fading from most of the Western Hemisphere. The Southern elite believed that slavery was vital to their economic success and were fiercely opposed to anything that would jeopardize their ability to profit at the hands of free labor. Abraham Lincoln, despite consistent concessions to the institution of slavery, threatened the delicate fabric of the South's economic core. Lincoln won the presidency in November 1860, despite having received not a single electoral vote from the South.

The Republican victory sent shockwaves throughout the South. Before Lincoln's inauguration, seven Southern states seceded from the Union and formed the Confederate States of America (CSA). The Louisiana Secession Convention consisted primarily of influential political and economic elites heavily invested in slavery. Only twenty-three parishes sent delegates, and the secessionist movement was led primarily by sugar cultivators. The delegates in Louisiana's secessionist convention "collectively owned more Negroes than any other political convention of equal number in the entire South." The delegates voted in favor of secession by a lopsided vote of 113 to 17 in January 1861. Antonio Marrero represented St. Bernard Parish and voted in line with economic interests of other planters in the parish. Louisiana governor Thomas Moore and the business community desired to make New Orleans a free and neutral city to ensure a safe flow of capital. Despite this goal, Louisiana succumbed to pressure from the planter elite and officially joined the Confederacy on March 21, 1861. A divided nation, and a divided state, mobilized for inevitable war.[52]

It's uncertain how whites from St. Bernard Parish reacted to Louisiana's secession from the United States and the resulting call to arms. Most had no personal stake in slavery and were not sympathetic to the ideals of the Anglo-American South. Some may have likely reacted in similar fashion to other Southern whites if they adopted the common mentality of the majority of white Anglo-Americans at the time. It is evident that although some Isleños men joined the Confederate army, most waited until the end of the war.

It's also uncertain how many whites from St. Bernard Parish joined the Confederate forces. The St. Bernard Mounted Rifles reported seventy-eight men. Wealthy slave owner Antonio Marrero organized an additional contingent of locals, and the Fifth Regiment of the Confederate Infantry contained Company B, the Chalmette Rifle Guards. Others joined lesser-known units as well.[53]

Many local whites joined the Chalmette Regiment, led by local planter Ignatius Szymanski. Szymanski, nicknamed "Colonel Ski," was a native of Poland with a lengthy military history. While in Poland, he had fought in the 1830 November Uprising that unsuccessfully attempted to expel the Russian Empire from Poland. In 1835, he immigrated to Louisiana, purchased land in St. Bernard Parish and married local socialite Charlotte Lacoste.[54]

The Isleños yielded to the demands of their newly formed nation, as they had with Spain during the American Revolution and with the United States during the War of 1812. As with most whites, many probably joined their local regiments for different reasons: ideologies on race, preservation of an institution that benefited them, a belief in states' rights or simply the belief that they were fighting for their homes and states. Overall, twenty thousand Louisiana whites enlisted for the war in the first nine months.[55]

On April 12, 1861, Confederate troops led by General Pierre Gustave Toutant "P.G.T." Beauregard fired on Fort Sumter, a Federally occupied fort in South Carolina. Lincoln responded with a call for troops to squash the rebellion. Arkansas, Virginia, Tennessee and North Carolina joined the Confederacy soon after, and the Civil War had officially begun.

Beauregard was a St. Bernard Parish native and a descendant of European nobility. He was a Creole who grew up on Contreras, a sugar cane plantation in lower St. Bernard Parish. His first languages were French and Spanish; he did not begin learning English until he was sent to school in New York City at age twelve. His military record was expansive prior to his entrance in the Civil War, as he'd been an engineer and captain during the Mexican-American War. Because of his fluency in Spanish, he was one of the first officers to enter Mexico City to administer its surrender. He briefly served as superintendent at West Point before resigning from the U.S. Army to serve his state with the newly established Confederacy.[56]

The site of the former Contreras Plantation, the birthplace of P.G.T. Beauregard. *Courtesy of Rhett Pritchard.*

Beauregard was among the wealthy planter class in the parish and was well known to the nearby Isleños. In June 1848, a party was thrown in St. Bernard Parish at the return of his arrival from the Mexican-American War. The *Daily Picayune* reported:

> *The inhabitants of the parishes of Plaquemines and St. Bernard regard with pride the able and honorable manner in which Lieut. Beauregard has fulfilled his duties as an officer of the Topographical Engineers in the American army, and the coolness, intrepidity and talents displayed by him in various battles in which he participated from Vera Cruz to Mexico.*[57]

New Orleans was an epicenter of global trade and by far the most populous city of the Confederacy. The city was vital for the South to protect and necessary for the Union to capture. Camp Chalmette, located on the grounds of the Battle of New Orleans, was commissioned in late 1861 to protect advancements from the river and provide supplementary training to troops. The camp had ten thirty-two-pound guns facing the river. Between the cannons and the river was a ditch approximately thirty feet wide and eight feet deep. One lieutenant stationed there proudly commented, "Woe be the Yankee that ever attempts to invade the Crescent City."[58]

Due to inactivity, there was an excess of leisure time at Camp Chalmette. Many troops passed the time by drinking heavily and playing poker, a game that originated in New Orleans. It was not unusual for men to sneak away from camp and take the short excursion to New Orleans for a night of drinking, gambling and visiting brothels. If they were caught upon arrival at Camp Chalmette, a strike to the face with a rifle by an officer was a common punishment.[59]

Two main forts in lower Plaquemines Parish, Fort Jackson and Fort St. Philip, were stockpiled with cannons to thwart a Union attack. Fort St. Philip notably resisted nine days of British bombardment in 1815. Fort Jackson, named after Andrew Jackson, was built in 1822 to create additional protection for New Orleans in case of another invasion attempt by a foreign enemy.

THE WAR IMMEDIATELY impacted the South's economy, and special laws passed in response to the war disproportionately impacted many poor, rural whites in favor of wealthy plantation owners. Slave owners who owned more than twenty slaves were exempt from drafts, while other wealthy men were legally permitted to purchase substitutes to fight in their place. Higher taxes on agricultural produce were felt hardest among poor farmers as opposed to large plantation owners. Inflation caused prices of basic necessities to skyrocket.[60]

These issues created backlash and resistance among some whites, who began to view the war as a rich man's war. Many whites in St. Bernard Parish and throughout rural areas in Louisiana, especially those living on the water's edge, started to ignore the new pleas of conscription from the Confederacy. Resistance was particularly high among Acadian communities throughout southern Louisiana. As the war continued, desertion increased among Confederate ranks.[61]

INVASION

The Union invaded New Orleans and the surrounding area in 1862. Unlike the British, the Union would not arrive via the lakes and bayous but attacked directly through the river. David Farragut was chosen to lead the largest naval fleet ever assembled in U.S. history to date. Farragut, a son of a Revolutionary War veteran, had lived in New Orleans throughout most of his childhood. At nine years old, he joined the navy and fought against the British aboard the *Essex*. He was captured in Chile at the age of fourteen. Although there were doubts of his Union loyalty, Farragut was granted the enormous task of capturing his childhood home, now a heavily fortified major Confederate city.[62]

Farragut first blockaded New Orleans, and the Confederacy resisted in a struggle known as the Battle of the Head of Passes. The Confederacy withdrew upriver after unsuccessfully challenging the Union fleet. Notably, the nearby disturbances did not completely detract from New Orleanians' Mardi Gras celebrations. Residents held seven huge carnival balls, and parades meandered through crowded city streets, though street masking was banned for fear of Union spies. Although the city celebrated, economic stagnation and the knowledge of a massive Union fleet dampened moods. One newspaper claimed that the holiday had "passed off with a quietness probably never before known to New Orleans. No masks on the street, no revelry or intoxication, as is to be seen by the absence of all serious cases from our police records."[63]

On March 15, Major General Mansfield Lovell declared martial law in New Orleans and neighboring parishes, including St. Bernard Parish, just as Andrew Jackson had decades earlier. The martial law decree was deemed so draconian that the Louisiana governor submitted a grievance to Jefferson Davis, the president of the Confederacy, regarding the "persistent complaints" he had received from his constituents. Lovell's goal in declaring martial law had been to rule out sympathizers and to coerce all "white male residents" to take up arms. Three weeks after martial law was decreed, only 12,984 white males—a small minority of the demographic overall—had pledged oaths. Many had either realized the impending doom before them or were discontent with the Confederacy. Reports of "sabotage, trade with the enemy, and verbal dissent" were widespread.[64]

The turnout for Lovell's calls for conscription of all white males represented an enormous disappointment for the Confederacy. The *New Orleans Bee* claimed the region was run amok with "apathy and indifference" to the Confederate cause. Parishes were ordered to form militias of white men between the ages of eighteen and forty-five. St. Bernard Parish, along with five other parishes in southern Louisiana, did not heed the call and sent no companies to New Orleans.[65]

The convergence of unique circumstances did not benefit the Confederacy, as these two forces were about to exchange blows. No matter the victor, the lasting repercussions would be felt harshest among the most vulnerable. Those repercussions would manifest themselves in a dangerous way in postwar St. Bernard Parish.

In April 1862, the Union fleet advanced upriver and attacked Fort St. Philip and Fort Jackson. Citizens from the parishes of St. Bernard and Plaquemines felt the relentlessness of the bombardment. According to Harnett T. Kane's *Deep Delta Country*, "Sun-darkened trappers and blue-clad oyster-tongers gazed at vessels—wooden gunboats and mortar schooners—such as they had never seen or imagined, sending high waves toward the shore, forcing small floods over the low-lying field here and there." Kane claimed houses collapsed from ricocheting cannonballs while some took to their boats to retreat to nearby islands as the battle raged. One local man noted that "it was like a big paw hitting at us, all the time."[66]

Albert Patterson, a former slave interviewed by the WPA in 1940, was tasked to carry the wounded to the hospital. He vividly recalled the attack:

> *I remember when de gunboats come up de river and took* [Fort] *Jackson and St. Phillip's Fort, and General Butler took New Orleans* [May 1, 1862]. *I seen some bad things. I seen de Rebel soldiers run wid their leg 'most cut off to de knee, or de arm hangin', de blood pourin'. De Colonel, he make me carry dem in de buggy so they could come here to de hospital. And then some of them start cussin', and insist they goin' right back to de battlefield even with their arm cut off so they can't carry a gun.*[67]

Many of the enslaved in St. Bernard Parish probably considered the Union fleet as a liberating force. If not liberation, the Union fleet provided aspirations for a better life, a life of hope free of servitude and bondage. Most probably recognized the Union occupiers would not bring complete jubilation but would perhaps usher a new wave of progress for black Americans that had been historically denied in the South. This mentality was in stark contrast to many of their white neighbors, especially the wealthy slave-owning elite.

On April 24, after skirmishes with both forts, Farragut's fleet triumphantly proceeded upriver to New Orleans. The Union fleet easily overpowered the Confederate fleet tasked with defending the city. According to John D.

Winters in *The Civil War in Louisiana*, "Self-destruction, lack of co-operation, cowardice of untrained officers, and the murderous fire of the Federal gunboats reduced the fleet to a demoralized shambles." One of the first Union vessels to anchor coerced a camp of Confederates led by Ignatius Szymanski to surrender. In total, the Union lost thirty-nine men and the Confederacy lost eleven.[68]

Desertion was common in nearby forts as word spread of the Union victory. An all-out mutiny occurred at Fort Jackson, in which lower-ranked soldiers forced the officers to surrender. The city itself was in havoc. The Confederacy burned bales of cotton and sugar and other valuable supplies. Mobs took advantage of the chaos and looted. Molasses dumped from the port flooded Canal Street. Some Confederate supporters lined the levees and fearlessly cursed the docking Union ships. Farragut ordered two officers to administer the surrender. George Washington Cable, a famed novelist from New Orleans, witnessed the event and wrote: "So through the gates of death those two men walked to the City Hall to demand the town's surrender. It was one of the bravest deeds I ever saw done." An overwhelmed Mansfield Lovell did not officially surrender, but he evacuated all Confederate troops within his power. The decision spared New Orleans the brutal destruction faced by other Southern cities.[69]

The capitulation of New Orleans was a major turning point for the war. The Confederacy lost its largest city and its robust industry and lavish revenues. Most importantly, it surrendered vital access to the mouth of the Mississippi River. South Louisiana was one of the Union's first major strongholds of the Civil War. The Confederacy would never recover from the loss.

RECENTLY ABANDONED CONFEDERATE camps in the area were converted into Union camps. Union troops took over Camp Chalmette on January 5, 1863. Perhaps the most detailed account of Camp Chalmette is from the diary of Lawrence Van Alstyne, a Union soldier. He noticed the quick withdrawal of Confederate troops upon arrival to the camp:

> *We have put up our tents, and have been looking about. It is a large camp ground and from all signs was lately occupied and was left in a hurry. Odds and ends of camp furniture are scatted about, and there are many signs of a hasty leave-taking. A few of us went back across the country to a large woods, where we found many trees covered with long gray mass, hanging*

down in a great bunches from the branches. We took all we could carry to make a bed of, for it is soft as feathers.[70]

He subsequently noted the doctor would not allow them to use the moss for bedding because it caused sickness. Alstyne was ecstatic to be on the grounds where the Battle of New Orleans was fought. He wrote a short entry about the celebration on January 8, 1863, the anniversary of the battle, and the sickness of the camp to perform drill: "To-day is the anniversary of the battle of New Orleans and is celebrated here like the Fourth of July at home. Drill has been attempted, but only about 200 men were fit for it and our camp duties are about all we are able to do."[71]

The conditions at Camp Chalmette were brutal. Alstyne frequently referenced his cough in his journal. On January 17, he noted a suicide attempt, the first of many, in which he intervened to save a life. Two days later, smallpox was discovered, and the carrier was isolated and left to die. On January 27, he wrote about the death of a friend who had kept "up the spirits" of Camp Chalmette: "Brown died this forenoon and I shall never forget the scene. He was conscious and able to talk and the last he said was for us to stick and hang. 'But boys,' said he, 'if I had the power, I would start north with all who wanted to go and as soon as we passed over four feet of ground I would sink it.'"[72]

Disease and death ravaged Camp Chalmette. The conditions were unbearable. Nonetheless, after the fall of New Orleans to the hands of the Union, African Americans quickly offered their military services to Major General Benjamin Butler. The First Louisiana Native Guard, initially a Confederate unit that saw no action, was the Union's first formally sanctioned all-black unit. The regiment included runaway slaves and free men of color. Although the Confederacy in Louisiana did not utilize any African American troops in combat, the Union used the troops during the Siege at Port Hudson. It was the first usage of African American troops in the Union army, three months prior to the famous Massachusetts Fifty-Fourth at the Second Battle of Fort Wagner. Port Hudson, the last Confederate stronghold in Louisiana, was the concluding engagement by the Union to fully capture the Mississippi River in Louisiana. By the end of the Civil War, over twenty-four thousand black Louisianans had joined the ranks of the Union. Seven thousand white men from Louisiana also enlisted in the Union army, more than the number of whites who enlisted in the Union army from North Carolina, Alabama, Texas, Florida or Georgia. Louisiana was a deeply divided state.[73]

One of the recently freedmen to join the Union army was Ceceil George's father. George told the story of a white man who approached with news about the events that led her father to fight:

> In de field de people was workin' and my uncle was de driver. We was in de road playin', and de man got to like the corner. We say, "Who dat comin'?" When he got close we break and run to the quarters. He say, "Don' run! Come back! I am yo' friend. How yo' all do?" But we ready to run, an' he reached in his sack, break up some "hard tack," dey call it, an' give us all a piece. When he done, he wrote on a piece of paper an' give it to my uncle, de driver. Den he say to us, "Can yo' keep a secret an' don' repeat?" We say, "Yes, sah." He say, "I come from yo' friend Abraham Lincoln. He say 'hold yo' peace.'" He took de map of de parish, an' I don't know when he walked back—maybe at night—but we don' see him no more.
>
> Den my father run off de plantation to de barracks to go to war. He was killed three months before we knew it, an' was buried in Chalmette. After that a uncle brought us up, and we had to stay in that heathen place till freedom come.[74]

The Union victory and the tide of the war in favor of the Union promised hope for the enslaved. Insubordination from those locked in bondage was rife. In April 1862, tensions rose between laborers and the overseers at the Millaudon Plantation in lower St. Bernard Parish due to grave disagreements on how harsh overseers should punish the laborers as Union troops occupied the region. Henry Clement Millaudon, the son of the plantation owner, paid a visit to George Windberry, the supposed "ringleader" inciting insubordination among the workforce. Millaudon lashed at Windberry with his whip, but to his dismay, Windberry struck back and caused Millaudon to fall. Windberry then fled to the cane fields after Millaudon fired a few rounds from his pistol. Millaudon gave William MacKay, the tough overseer, strict orders to use lethal force to establish order if necessary. The next day, MacKay shot two men who would not comply. He later attempted to shoot Freeman Washington, a slave, for the same reason, but Washington was armed and shot MacKay dead. Over 150 of Millaudon's enslaved workforce abandoned the site en masse in search of freedom. The Millaudon family eventually abandoned its property.[75]

The events at Millaudon Plantation were not an anomaly. Thousands abandoned nearby plantations via any transportation available in Union-occupied territory in hopes of freedom. One planter referenced the departure of the enslaved in his journal as a "perfect stampede." By the summer of 1862, hundreds of the formally enslaved amassed in Union camps, including Camp Chalmette, while planters demanded back what they considered their rightful property. The issue compelled the Union government to adopt policies to address the situation.[76]

Major General Benjamin Butler devised a compromise to appease both the recently freed and their old slave owners. Butler needed the cooperation of former slave owners to establish a reliable government and reap the profitable benefits of the local agricultural economy. In 1859, over 60 percent "of all sugar made in the United States that year" came from the sugar-producing region surrounding New Orleans. In St. Bernard and Plaquemines Parishes, freedpeople were to return to their plantations and planters were to pay fair wages. Planters consented to pay a monthly wage of ten dollars, and if the planter provided basic necessities, he had the right to deduct three dollars. Women were paid less.[77]

Under these new contract agreements, laborers had to work ten hours a day for twenty-six days per month. Butler outlawed corporal punishment from the planters, but in order to appease their requests, he provided plantations with Union soldiers to oversee discipline and ensure

Fleeing from the Land of Bondage.—On the Mississippi River in 1863. Recently emancipated African Americans board a steamboat as a Union soldier stands guard. *Courtesy of the New Orleans Historic Collection.*

Plantation police checking the papers of freedpeople in St. Bernard Parish in 1863. Movement for freedpeople was limited even after the abolishment of slavery. *Courtesy of the Library of Congress.*

laborers stayed on the plantation. The formally enslaved soon realized some of the new occupiers were cracking the same whips they hoped to escape. Butler acknowledged the claims of slaveholders while providing token rights to the recently freed and appeasing those who questioned the institution of slavery. The plan benefited ex-slaveholders more than the recently freed. In many cases, conditions were probably not much different than slavery.[78]

On January 1, 1863, less than a year after the Union capture of New Orleans, Abraham Lincoln issued the Emancipation Proclamation to abolish slavery in the South. The proclamation exempted federally occupied parts of Louisiana, including "the Parishes of St. Bernard, Plaquemines." Although slavery was legally allowed to persist, Butler's plan already addressed the situation, at least temporarily.[79]

Throughout the remainder of the war, there was seemingly no resistance from St. Bernard Parish. Many plantation owners either left or adapted to the new system, which still allowed for significant profit. Antonio Marrero abandoned his plantation and rented his land to freedmen. According to 1865 tax roll reports, Marrero was still the wealthiest Isleño in the parish. Radical Republicans—dubbed "carpetbaggers" by local Democrats, a pejorative for Northerners who moved to the South during or after the Civil War—purchased and operated some of the plantations.[80]

The lack of resistance spared St. Bernard Parish any destruction. Resistance in other regions resulted in complete devastation. The once thriving town of Donaldsonville in Ascension Parish was reduced to rubble, and numerous plantations were set ablaze by the Union military due to Confederate partisans resisting occupation.[81]

AFTER THE WAR, many of St. Bernard Parish's famous participants returned distraught. P.G.T. Beauregard pledged an oath to the Union and was pardoned for his participation. He was asked to serve in multiple foreign armies: Brazil, Romania and Egypt. He declined all and stated he would rather be forgotten in his home country than given riches to fight for another. He lived a postwar life engaged with engineering and politics. He oversaw General Robert E. Lee's funeral but refused to attend the funeral of Jefferson Davis due to personal differences.[82]

Ignatius Szymanski returned to his plantation in Terre-aux-Boeufs, Sebastopol, which still stands today. He started a successful cotton press business that operated on the corner of Clouet and Levee Streets in New

Sebastopol Plantation, home of Ignatius Szymanski. *Courtesy of Rhett Pritchard.*

The renovated house of Albert Estopinal at the Los Isleños Heritage and Multi-Cultural Museum. *Author's collection.*

Orleans. Despite a defeat at Union hands, Szymanski and others did not face substantial losses.[83]

Albert Estopinal, a wealthy Isleño, was another important Confederate veteran from St. Bernard Parish. At seventeen, he quit school to enlist and, because of his education, was immediately promoted to sergeant of his company. He fought in many battles, including the decisive Battle of Vicksburg, which resulted in a Union victory. The result divided the Confederacy and granted the Union the necessary conditions for a victory at Port Hudson. Although not to the extent of the Battle of Gettysburg, the Battle of Vicksburg is considered a major turning point of the Civil War. After the war, Estopinal began a colorful political career that led to his election as a United States representative.[84]

The Civil War had dire consequences for the Louisiana economy. It nearly halted sugar cane production throughout the sugar cane region. Production in Louisiana fell from 110,500 tons of sugar prior to the war to 6,000 tons in

1864. Competition increased from Cuba, Hawaii and other regions where cheap labor was abundant and the climate was optimal. The industry took decades to return to its prewar output.[85]

The Civil War significantly altered the social, political and economic structure of St. Bernard Parish. Poor rural whites did not fare well after the war. Employment opportunities were slim, wages were low, prices were high and newfound competition ignited already existing racial tension. The Civil War impaired some of the privileges previously enjoyed by whites, as many whites viewed Reconstruction as an unnecessary occupation that favored freedpeople and disparaged their way of life. Freedpeople were scapegoated and received the brunt of the blame. Newspapers owned by planters or business elites invested in slavery were consistently full of anti-Republican and racial propaganda. Illiterate whites, such as most of the poor whites in St. Bernard Parish, heard rhetoric from wealthy elites that made them fear freedpeople or regard them as inferior. They were told their economic hardships were the fault of their black counterparts. The business community exploited their economic distress and fears and organized them in Democratic clubs. One St. Bernard Parish politician later testified, "I know some of the richest merchants here in New Orleans who subscribed large sums of money towards organizing and getting up these different clubs." This racist mentality coupled with distressed economic conditions led to a dangerous instability. The conditions were ripe for tensions to escalate.[86]

Chapter 3

ESCALATION

Vallvey Veillon shot him with a pistol killing him dead.
—a freedman's testimony of a murder

In 1863, as the Civil War raged, President Lincoln took a moderate stance on normalizing relations with states that seceded. In Louisiana, he proposed a lenient plan to bring the state back into the Union; his plan granted immediate amnesty to Rebels who pledged their loyalty to the Union. Under this plan, freedpeople were to be paid at least ten dollars a month on plantations. Lastly, in order for Louisiana to be admitted back into the Union, only 10 percent of the state's electorate had to pledge the loyalty oath, and the state's new constitution must abolish slavery.

In 1864, Lincoln's plan was put into effect in Louisiana, but not without great objection. Louisiana sent two senators and five representatives to Washington. Congress, controlled by Radical Republicans with deep animosity toward the South, refused to acknowledge their votes as protest toward Lincoln's plan. In addition, many of the nation's prominent figures, including Fredrick Douglass, opposed the plan.

Reconstruction in the South ushered a new wave of opportunities for previously enslaved people. In 1865, the Thirteenth Amendment, the first of the three Reconstruction amendments, formally abolished slavery. Louisiana was the second ex-Confederate state to ratify it, following Virginia. Furthermore, the federal government also established the Bureau of Refugees, Freedmen and Abandoned Lands, usually referred to as the

An agent from the Freedmen's Bureau stopping a conflict between armed white and black groups. *Harper's Weekly*, 1868. *Courtesy of the Library of Congress.*

Freedmen's Bureau, to aid freedpeople and some white refugees. It was designed to help freedpeople find lost loved ones, expand education, assist with employment and provide desperately needed legal representation. Although the Freedmen's Bureau had a positive impact, black Louisianans still experienced discrimination in every facet of daily life, and racial tensions remained high.

In St. Bernard Parish, freedpeople took immediate advantage of these new prospects. Jean Pierre Fazende, a free man of color and successful merchant, inherited a stretch of land from the Chalmette Plantation on the grounds where the Battle of New Orleans occurred. In 1856, his son subdivided the land and sold thirty-three lots to other free people of color. After the Civil War, the opportunity to buy land was also presented to freedpeople.[87]

The residents of this community, "Fazendeville," were proud of their history and felt a close connection to it. They even named their church Battle Ground Baptist Church. Although similar to other African American communities, it was unique in a parish that would eventually become predominately white in the twentieth century. The community consisted of dozens of families, complete with a barroom, a baseball field, a grocery store and a one-room schoolhouse. It thrived for over a century.[88]

Despite monumental gains by freedpeople, they continued to face state-sanctioned discrimination. Shortly after the end of the Civil War, the Louisiana legislature and parish governments passed a series of laws that disproportionately impacted people of color, known collectively as Black Codes. The Black Codes reversed many improvements granted by the federal government. African Americans were stripped of or denied several rights: housing options were severely limited, carrying weapons or anything that could be identified as such was prohibited, labor contracts closely resembled slavery and vagrancy was outlawed, but a "good behavior" clause was enacted for these laws for the possibility of racial interpretation. The strict policing and the incarceration of freedpeople provided employers with free labor, as the Thirteenth Amendment created an exception to slavery in which the government was sanctioned to use prisoners as free labor.[89]

Violence toward freedpeople continued in St. Bernard Parish after the Civil War. On Christmas Day 1866, Washington Rehan, a freedman, was boasting to his friend at a local bar about purchasing a pistol. This was quite the feat considering just a few years earlier Rehan was enslaved. Santiago Artialla, the bar owner, was appalled by a former slave owning a firearm. When Rehan set the pistol on the counter, Artialla picked it up, aimed it at Rehan and said, "Look out!" before discharging a bullet into Rehan's head. The coroner ruled death by accidental discharge. This individual act of hatred and brutality was merely a precursor to the impending violence.[90]

Beyond St. Bernard Parish, freedpeople experienced consistent violence throughout the region. On July 30, 1866, the Louisiana Constitutional Convention convened in part to address the enactment of the Black Codes and how it undermined Republican progress. White Democrats were suspicious of this convention and felt Republicans were attempting to solidify more power in New Orleans. As members of the convention exited, they were met by black marchers and a marching band. In contrast, a group of heavily armed whites, many of whom were veterans of the Confederate army bitter about their recent defeat, waited on the corner of Common and Dryades Streets.

It is unknown who shot first, but a battle between the two crowds ensued. The majority of the black marchers were unarmed and sought refuge in a nearby building. The white mob relentlessly attacked the black marchers who attempted to retreat. Eventually, federal troops regained order and martial law was declared. Many of the white rioters were jailed. The exact death toll varies depending on the source. It is estimated between thirty-four to over one hundred, the majority of whom were African American.[91]

The calamity, along with a similar event in Memphis, created national outrage toward white southerners and the Democratic Party. Three months after the riot, the Republicans gained a sizable majority in both houses of Congress. They worked to pass the Fourteenth Amendment, officially adopted in 1868, which granted citizenship to freedpeople, and other measures that established stronger federal military oversight of vast areas of the South.

THESE NEW LEGAL rights allowed Republicans, the overwhelming majority of whom were freedpeople, to better organize in St. Bernard Parish. In 1867, over nine hundred people gathered at the residence of freedman Leopold Guichard. Prominent black Republican C.C. Morgan spoke at the event. The *New Orleans Tribune*, a historic bilingual African American newspaper founded in 1864, documented his speech in an article covering the event:

> *Fellow citizens, I thank God that after centuries of slavery the hour has at last come when you are freemen and the principles of Thomas Jefferson are not only acknowledged to be correct in theory, but are about to be put to a practical test; your enemies, the enemies of human progress, have declared that the natural condition of the black race is that of servitude, that no good can come out of Africans except as "hewers of wood and drawers of water," and therefore, that you ought to be slaves; that you are incapable of receiving education, even where you have the opportunity; that you will not work except under the lash. Let us answer these declarations in their order if as they say your natural condition is one of servitude, is it not a little singular that you accepted unanimously the liberty which the immortal Lincoln offered you, and that there is not a black man or woman on the face of the earth who is willing to return to slavery. If as they say you are incapable of receiving education, why is it, I ask, that so many thousands of our race who knew not one letter of the alphabet before the rebellion are now able to read and write. If while slaves you were sunk into the lowest depths of ignorance, whose fault was it who made the laws which declared it a crime to teach the poor slave his ABC's. If as they say, you are idle vagabonds and will not work except under the lash, I ask you but to look around you now that the lash dare not be used, and judge for yourselves who are the idle, the thriftless rebel loafers, whose occupation of whipping niggers is gone. Now my friends, you are not only freedmen but you are citizens of the United States, voters, and as such, responsible for your acts. Prove to the world that you are worthy of taking part in the government of this great country, that your oppressors have belied you, that you have intelligence to discriminate between a bad man and a good one, you know the difference between a rebel and a Union man, and when you come to elect candidates for the coming election, which is shortly to take place, see that you elect good, loyal men, who have always been your friends, and will support the rights of our race.*
> *Ask of those who want your vote what they have done for the cause; whether in the times that tried men's souls, they abandoned the protection*

of the Stars and Stripes and took protection under the bastard flag of barbarism, the flag of the Confederacy. If they did, turn your back upon them, and vote for those who were willing to sacrifice all for the sake of the Union, whose hearts were heavy when they heard of a rebel victory and leaped with joy when Farragut and Butler came to the rescue. Vote for those who on the battle-field stared death in the face for their country's sake, vote for those who suffered in rebel prisons, for your sake and for mine, and, finally, vote for men who are honest, capable, and loyal to the Government.[92]

The meeting ended with the "wildest enthusiasm." A month later, the *New Orleans Tribune* requested letters from Republican officials throughout Louisiana to report on the violent disturbances between Republicans and Democrats. Guichard sent in his letter: "Sir—In the parish of St. Bernard everything is progressing well. Our club has been formed since the 12th of May, 1867. We are progressing very well and have not, as yet, been interfered with or threatened. I am under the impression that we owe our escape from interference to our close proximity to the city."[93]

Freedpeople not only organized politically; they also organized for better working conditions as they became more accustomed to noncoercive labor. They continued to be protected by federal troops and quickly realized their labor was in dire need by planters. Despite elevated tensions, in 1867, white planters in St. Bernard and Plaquemines Parishes agreed to pay twelve dollars a month with rations and eighteen dollars a month to the hardest and most successful laborers. However, freedpeople exercised their rights to leave in search of better wages, causing the idea of a uniform wage rate to dissipate. Some monthly wages rose to fifteen and twenty dollars, respectively. In May 1868, laborers around the area organized and went on strike for better wages. Laborers exploited the times of high harvest, as any delay would financially destabilize planters. However, when labor needs were low, there were instances of planters firing freedpeople in St. Bernard Parish for attending Republican meetings.[94]

African Americans in St. Bernard Parish also exercised their newly granted voting rights. In April 1868, Louisiana ratified a new constitution by 58 percent to 42 percent due to the votes of freedpeople. St. Bernard Parish voted in favor by 55 percent to 45 percent. The Louisiana Constitution of 1868 was one of the most progressive constitutions in the South. It abolished the Black Codes, granted African Americans equal access to public accommodations and even attempted to integrate public schools. While theoretically progressive, it did little to end racial discrimination.[95]

Oscar J. Dunn, lieutenant governor of Louisiana, seated in the middle and surrounded by twenty-nine portraits of African American delegates to the Louisiana Constitution of 1868. *Courtesy of the Library of Congress.*

Left: Henry Warmoth, circa 1870. *Courtesy of Library of Congress.*

Right: A cartoon attempting to link the Democratic Party with the Confederate cause. The Confederate flag was exchanged for a "Seymour & Blair" sign; a CSA (Confederate States of America) hat was exchanged for a KKK hat. *Harper's Weekly*, 1868. *Courtesy of the Library of Congress.*

St. Bernard Parish also helped elect twenty-six-year-old Republican governor Henry Clay Warmoth and Lieutenant Governor Oscar Dunn by 65.5 percent. Warmoth, a Union veteran, was one of the youngest governors to be elected in United States history and had a keen interest in black suffrage. Dunn, a former slave, was the first African American lieutenant governor in the country. He died while in office in 1871 and had one of the largest funerals in Louisiana history; an estimated fifty thousand people lined Canal Street for his procession. He was succeeded by Pinckney Benton Stewart Pinchback, who fought with the First Louisiana Native Guard during the Civil War. Pinchback went on to become the country's first African American governor. It was not until the election of Douglas Wilder of Virginia in 1990 that the United States saw another African American governor. Local politics also changed due to the voting power of people of color. Dr. A.G. Thornton, a white physician and known Republican, was elected parish judge. St. Bernard Parish was well underway in becoming a Republican stronghold and perturbing the established political and economic status quo.[96]

In July 1868, with Republican control solidified and the Fourteenth Amendment ratified, Louisiana was readmitted into the Union. This Republican dominance intensified the upcoming presidential election of 1868, which was to be held on November 3. Democrats of St. Bernard Parish were fuming at the harsh realization of being a minority without political dominance. The ticket options consisted of Republican and famed Union veteran Ulysses S. Grant against Democrat Horatio Seymour, former governor of New York. Whites in Louisiana had much to gain with a Seymour victory; Seymour vehemently opposed Reconstruction policies and believed in stronger autonomy for states. He appealed to the vast racism of the country for votes. He labeled Grant the "Nigger" candidate and painted himself as the "White Man's" candidate. It was obvious St. Bernard Parish, along with Louisiana, would vote Republican unless Democrats could hinder the black vote. A Seymour victory meant the end of federal occupation. The stakes were high.

In April 1868, Republicans held a meeting while Democrats held a barbecue. The *Daily Picayune* reported a harrowing account, although the details are potentially misconstrued given the newspaper's political sentiments. At the Republican meeting, Henry Clay Warmoth and other prominent Republicans spoke. Some freedmen participated in the Democratic barbecue, and a black preacher was scheduled to speak at the event. Freedmen participating in the Democratic barbecue angered black Republicans. Black Republicans, some of whom were armed, went to the barbecue waving the U.S. flag to anger ex-Confederates and their sympathizers. Tensions escalated, and the Republicans shot one black attendee and beat others. The preacher refused to speak under such conditions. Gunfire was exchanged, and freedmen and whites from nearby joined the fight before the groups dispersed.[97]

Both parties continued to hold meetings and rallies as the election drew nearer. Given St. Bernard Parish's racial makeup and political instability, it was a hotbed for partisan activism. Democrats frequently held their meetings without any more interference from the Republicans. Prominent Democrats such as General James B. Steedman spoke at several rallies, while Republicans, on the other hand, gathered less frequently as threats and intimidation tactics increased. According to First Lieutenant Jesse Matlock Lee, the Freedmen's Bureau officer tasked with investigating the massacre, Republican "meetings were generally looked upon by the opposite party as a toleration, not a right. Certain white men residing in the Parish, who were leaders of the Republicans, were threatened with assassination."[98]

On September 27, Republicans and Democrats both held a meeting in close vicinity. The Democrats hosted a meeting at Antonio Marrero's plantation and advertised "free whiskey and free meat." Governor Warmoth and other notable politicians spoke at the Republican meeting. After the Republican meeting, their procession passed the Millaudon Plantation, which had been abandoned since the Civil War and its ex–slave quarters rented to freedpeople. At the plantation, armed white men from the Democratic meeting sent a freedman and freedwoman under their authority, most likely without their consent, to the roadside to taunt the procession as it passed. It was the hope of the Democrats that the Republicans would be provoked by the two insulting them, thus providing justification for the Democrats to attack the procession. The plot was foiled, as the Republicans suspected the motivation behind the jeers. A local planter remarked that incident as the "first disturbance."[99]

After the procession, Governor Warmoth went to dinner at a sugar plantation owned by Thomas Ong, the white Republican chairman of the board of registrars in St. Bernard Parish. Ong moved to the area in 1862 to become a profitable planter and was considered a carpetbagger by local whites. He was an influential Republican leader who held various political positions. He was elected as a delegate in the parish and participated in the constitutional convention of 1864. Although he was a Radical Republican, a Democratic-leaning newspaper claimed he was an "esteemed" member of the community because of his business dealings. In 1868, he employed forty-five freedpeople at his plantation. During his later testimony to Congress, Ong disclosed that he noticed numerous carts full of large quantities of hay pass by his residence as the Democrats met on October 11, 1868. He learned afterward "that the hay concealed their arms," many of which were double-barreled shotguns. Ong and other Republican leaders wanted to host more meetings and processions but decided against it as the climate grew more precarious.[100]

Rumors escalated that white Democrats would resort to violence to ensure a political victory in November. Republican and Union veteran H.N. Whittemore, the parish's Freedmen's Bureau agent at the time, received information that Sheriff Antoine Chalaire was going to disarm freedpeople and possibly murder any freedmen found armed. Whittemore told the freedpeople to give him their arms to avoid bloodshed, and he would return the weapons to them once the excitement from the election

Kenilworth Plantation, home to Thomas Ong during the massacre. *Courtesy of Rhett Pritchard.*

subsided. Although his intentions were pure and perhaps this maneuver helped temporarily prevent violence, it left many freedpeople unarmed and defenseless at a time when violence was imminent.[101]

On Saturday, October 24, Democrats concocted plans to assassinate Ong and another prominent Republican leader, General Albert Lindley Lee, both of whom purchased property after the Civil War and often protected and employed freedpeople. General A.L. Lee, originally from New York, was serving as a justice on the Kansas Supreme Court until the start of the Civil War. He joined the Union army in 1861 and was quickly promoted to brigadier general in 1862. He was instrumental throughout many Union victories in the South. After the Civil War, General Lee purchased property in lower St. Bernard Parish, involved himself with local politics and became an editor for Republican newspapers in New Orleans. His profile made him a prime target. The would-be assassins also extended their list to Judge Thornton and a renowned member of the Metropolitan Police, Mike Curtis. Curtis was a Union veteran tasked with maintaining peace in the parish. Susan Clarke, a freedwoman, overheard these plans and notified the potential victims. Another freedman also overheard similar conversations and personally awoke Ong from his sleep

Albert Lindley Lee, circa 1860s.
Courtesy of the Library of Congress.

to notify him of the impending doom. Curtis's home was surrounded that night by ten to fifteen potential attackers, but Curtis was armed and expecting them. No assassination attempts were made.[102]

The next day, Sunday, October 25, racial tensions escalated and violence imploded. The Democratic clubs of St. Bernard Parish, the Constitutionalists and the Bumble-Bees, assembled at Millaudon Plantation. They were accompanied by the Seymour Innocents, a group of mostly Sicilian toughs from New Orleans, and the Seymour Infantus, bodyguards of Seymour Innocents. According to Ten Tennell in *Crucible of Reconstruction: War, Radicalism, and Race in Louisiana, 1861–1877*, the Seymour Infantus and the Innocents were "secret paramilitary political clubs and societies" organized to thwart Republican governments, especially through violence. Both societies were present in large numbers in St. Bernard Parish during election time. They arrived by steamboat from New Orleans and joined the other clubs in procession down the road to the courthouse and then toward the St. Bernard Catholic Church to have their flags consecrated by an officiating priest. The procession was led by Vallvey Veillon, Mr. Barrose,

St. Bernard Catholic Church. *Author's collection.*

St. Bernard Highway in lower St. Bernard Parish, the road leading to the events of the massacre. *Courtesy of Rhett Pritchard.*

Francis Estopinal and other hard-lined Democrats. Veillon seemed to be the ringleader throughout much of the start of the violence.[103]

After stopping at the church, the procession was returning to the courthouse when they saw Eugene Lock, a freedman, on the road. Members of the procession yelled for Lock to pull off his "hat and hurrah for Seymour and Blair." Lock refused and stood firm as they threatened him. One man grabbed ahold of Lock to intimidate him into cheering for Seymour. Lock remained steadfast. His refusal to cheer stimulated the indignation of the procession. Suddenly, one man lunged at Lock with a knife and another shot at him. In retaliation, Lock drew his revolver and fired at his assailants, hitting one man in the shoulder. Shots were fired, and Lock desperately tried to escape by climbing a picket fence. Veillon, who was on horseback and armed with a shotgun, easily closed in on Lock and delivered a fatal shot to the head. Another member of the procession pierced a lifeless Lock with a knife three times to ascertain his death.[104]

One freedman, known only as Cyrus in his testimonies, gave his testimony of the events to Lieutenant J.M. Lee:

They came into Mr. Turner's yard where I was living at the time, came up to Eugene, who lived there, Eugene was running from the men getting on the picket fence. Vallvey Veillon shot him with a pistol killing him dead. The other man had a dirk and ran after the colored man—Eugene—struck at him three times at the fence.

Cyrus saw Veillon the day he gave his testimony. Another freedman, Henry Sterling, was wounded at the same time Lock was killed. After the murder, Veillon went to Millaudon Plantation to wash the blood off his hands and reload his shotgun. He remarked that he was ready to "kill twenty more damned niggers." The first blood was spilled.[105]

Chapter 4

CULMINATION

*They are coming to kill you, we know it,
and we are going to protect you and your family.*
—*an unknown freedman*

Vallvey Veillon tasted blood early that Sunday morning and wanted more. After his posse washed themselves of the blood from their first victim at the Millaudon Plantation, they came across Spencer Jones, an unsuspecting elderly freedman going about his daily work. Veillon did not like Jones watching them wash off their blood. Veillon said, "I'll kill you. What are you looking at?" Jones replied, "I am doing nothing but standing here." The answer did not suffice for Veillon. Veillon rammed him with his horse and slit his throat in one swift stroke with a large bowie knife. Although Veillon was armed with a gun, he perhaps chose a knife to make the slaughter more personal. Jones, badly wounded, barely escaped Veillon's grip and fled.[106]

The actions of Veillon and his crew gained traction among other white residents. On the same plantation, Antonio Gonzales, a young white man, approached Jane Ackus, a freedwoman. Gonzales knocked her down and started kicking her. Ackus pleaded for mercy. Another man approached and said, "If she moves or opens her mouth again, knock her." Ackus stayed still and silent to survive. She would not be as fortunate two days later.[107]

A seemingly quiet Sunday turned into mayhem. Word spread quickly throughout the parish that the horrors envisioned were coming to fruition.

Freedwomen in nearby plantations dropped their bundles and fled in sheer panic. It was believed that the threats of assassination of Republican leaders and the murder of "all radical niggers who would not vote the Democratic ticket" would become a reality.[108]

The armed procession passed Eugene Joseph, a freedman returning from New Orleans alone. Joseph knew nothing of the troubles of the parish. The procession told Joseph to yell "Hurrah for Seymour and Blair!" Joseph, realizing he was alone and sensing danger, took off his hat and "whirled it around a little." They responded, "Bully for you!" and continued on their path. Joseph, like Ackus, would also not be so fortunate during his next interaction.[109]

Dr. A.G. Thornton, the recently elected Republican judge, sent a summons to the parish sheriff upon hearing of these calamities but received no response. Later that Sunday evening, around thirty men approached Dr. Thornton's residence and yelled obscenities and death threats. Thornton's residence was boarded up, and he had no desire to meet the incensed men. Reports of the violence "up the road" quickly reached Thomas Ong's plantation. Ong sent Michael Curtis, the Metropolitan policeman, with a letter to Sheriff Chalaire requesting a restoration of order before the violence escalated. Ong was unaware Thornton had already attempted to reach Sheriff Chalaire for assistance.[110]

Curtis remarked on the difficulty of passing angry armed processions to reach his destination. Considering the geographical landscape of lower St. Bernard Parish, there were not many roads leading in and out of the area. Nonetheless, Curtis mounted one of Ong's many horses to meet with the sheriff. As Curtis passed an armed posse, someone yelled, "Death to the police!" Curtis initially lied and claimed he was not a Metropolitan policeman.[111]

According to one account, Curtis unwittingly yelled he was actually a police officer after he rode past the procession. Whether it was that admission, the desire to stop Curtis from reaching his destination to request assistance or something else entirely, it warranted the attention of the angry procession. The men drew their weapons and pursued Curtis. After multiple shots in his direction, Curtis yelled for the assailants to hold their fire. He jumped from his horse and tried to escape through the yard of Thornton and into his boarded residence. As he was in the process of hopping Thornton's wooden fence, a man by the name of Syes John Buiel shot him in the back of the head. His body immediately went limp, and he collapsed to the ground. Other men approached the lifeless body and shot him several times to ascertain his death.[112]

A few freedpeople who witnessed the murder of Mike Curtis decided to give him a proper burial. Dr. Tross, one of the freedpeople who attempted to bury Curtis, testified that as he was "pushing the dirt on him" he "heard the guns a cracking." He attempted to get the other freedpeople assisting in the burial to leave, but they did not believe they would be attacked burying a fallen man. Tross told them they are going to "kill everything in the quarters." Tross ran to the swamps and on to New Orleans for safety as the others did not heed his warning. He later returned to find out he was right. Pierre Colet was shot dead, and the other three had severe bullet wounds. Sophia Marshall, one of the freedwomen, barely survived a gunshot wound to her chest.[113]

The news of the murder of a Metropolitan police officer spread rapidly throughout the parish. The unfathomable act terrified the freedpeople. If angry Democrats could do that to an armed white police officer and experienced war veteran, then they could imagine their fate. According to a later testimony given by Ong, "The killing of that man greatly exasperated the blacks, as they knew that he was one of the men that had fought for their freedom." Curtis was a Union veteran who fought in "all the heavy-fought battles of Virginia" and often boasted about "having aided in having conquered the rebellion."[114]

Ong hoped the rumors were fallacious, but his hopes were laid to rest by an eyewitness. In another desperate attempt to halt the violence, Ong sent an elderly and unsuspicious freedman, John King, as a courier. He gave

A cartoon titled "One Less Vote" depicts a dead black man killed by racial violence to undermine a Republican victory. *Harper's Weekly*, 1868.

precise directions to take a circuitous route on foot to notify Thornton, get a horse and ride to Jackson Barracks, a military barracks in New Orleans not far from the St. Bernard Parish line, to request federal troops immediately to respond to the violence.[115]

King followed the instructions from Ong and left at eight o'clock that Sunday night. As he neared Thornton's residence, he ran into a group of about twenty armed white men. He heard them cock their guns and aim them in his direction. King froze in panic. They debated killing him until a cold voice remarked that he was "nobody but an old fool nigger, need not kill him." King found the horse Curtis rode earlier before his death and rode to the barracks as fast as the horse could muster. He gave them Ong's letter describing the parish as on the brink of "slaughter."[116]

The local government was too powerless, too fearful or too apathetic to stop the ensuing violence. The few Metropolitan Police officers servicing the parish were inadequate. For example, John B. Jacques was commissioned as a Metropolitan Police officer on October 19 and reported for duty in St. Bernard Parish the next day. He was warned by "several colored women" to stay away from the courthouse because Metropolitan Police officers were in danger of being killed. Jacques was detained by a posse a few days later for allegedly conspiring to kill Antonio Marrero. With little assistance from the federal government and no help from the local government, Thornton locked himself in his domicile in anticipation of an attack. Sheriff Chalaire was either too immobilized to act due to lack of support, as he would later claim, or complacent with the violence, as Republicans would later suggest. The newly elected justice of the peace fled to the cane fields for safety.[117]

By nightfall that Sunday, the freedpeople had started to mobilize, as they felt unprotected and abandoned by the government. Those who had not given their arms to Whittemore picked them up and prepared for battle. Others grabbed knives or even tools as weapons. By nine o'clock, over 150 freedmen had gathered around Ong's house. They yelled excitedly in Creole French. The atmosphere was tense. Ong, nervous about the potential outcome, went outside to address the angered gathering and analyze their motives. One freedman immediately said, "Mr. Ong, you must go back to the house, we don't want you out here with us. We want no white men here at all, we won't let any white man pass here." Another shouted, "They are coming to kill you, we know it, and we are going to protect you and your family."[118]

Ong told the crowd that this was not how they should protect him and that their presence would only give more justification for the violence against them. He told them to disperse, as fighting back would be ineffective.

Ong overheard plans that those gathered intended to go to the Millaudon Plantation to "make a stand." According to Ong, "It was generally believed… that they would be attacked that night, and that the fight was to commence then." The group headed up the road toward the Millaudon Plantation to "await the attack." Ong locked his doors and retreated into his domicile in hopes that King had reached Jackson Barracks. Ong heard dozens of shots not even twenty minutes later, followed by a blaze in the distance. A group of freedmen brought two wounded victims to his home shortly after the shots rang out.[119]

The cause of the shots, the fire and the wounded men was a scuffle between the freedpeople who left Ong's residence and Pablo San Feliu, a known racist with staunch anti-Republican political views. Feliu was a baker and also sold whiskey on the side. People of color frequented his residence to purchase his alcohol. A week before his death, Mike Curtis reported that Feliu threatened to "kill every Metropolitan policeman that passed there." Metropolitan policemen and employees of the Freedmen's Bureau all stayed clear of his residence. On Sunday, October 25, Feliu held a Democratic meeting and reportedly stated that the "white people present go that night to the houses of the colored people and shoot them down as they presented themselves at the door." His neighbors described him as a "very disagreeable" and "very quarrelsome" man who habitually let his oxen roam on the crops of other properties.[120]

The next course of events varies widely depending on the source. The majority of information obtained is from the aforementioned report by Lieutenant Jesse M. Lee, a lieutenant from the Freedmen's Bureau tasked with investigating the massacre. The testimonies of the survivors are essential in attempting to comprehend the complex series of events. Lee provides two different accounts but clearly favors one over the other.[121]

According to the first account, usually the narrative of white Democrats, over one hundred freedmen left Ong's plantation armed and organized. They attacked Feliu's residence without provocation and killed him because he would not provide them with whiskey. After, they set fire to his home. Some even suggested Ong sent the group to carry out the murder.[122]

The second account, told by black and white Republicans, is the one Lee favored. According to this account, as the freedmen were leaving Ong's residence, they stopped at Feliu's to buy whiskey. Feliu, aware of the surrounding violence and the intentions of the freedmen, appeared at the window and fired his shotgun toward those closest to his home. Before reloading, he picked up another shotgun and fired, wounding several freedmen. Two wounded men were rushed to Thomas Ong's plantation for assistance. Feliu repeated the process with multiple guns. After at least twenty shots, there was a pause, perhaps to reload, and it provided the freedmen the opportunity to ambush his residence. Feliu killed the first intruder, Thompson Morgan, before falling victim to multiple gunshot wounds. The freedmen looted and then set fire to his home, burning the bodies of both Feliu and Morgan.[123]

Lee gives credence to the second account in his report. He claims:

> *I give it as my opinion after the most careful and patient inquiry in relation to this matter, that the attack on Pablo Felio [sic] was not premeditated on the part of the freedmen, or any one else, that they did not attack his house until after he had fired into them: that he fired the first shots, wounding several freedmen—shedding the first blood, and that [had] he acted with any degree of judgment or presence of mind, neither himself or his house would have been injured by the freedmen.[124]*

Although Lee believes the second version to be more accurate, he claims to be "at a loss to understand why one man would fire into a hundred freedmen, the greater number of whom were armed." For unstated reasons in any of the accounts, the freedmen dispersed after the incident with Feliu, perhaps realizing they could not muster an adequate defense against mounted men armed with shotguns.[125]

Louis Wilson, a freedman who gave his testimony to Lieutenant J.M. Lee, was with the group that night. According to Wilson, who referred to Feliu as "Mr. Powells," the events transpired as such:

> *We started up about dark, when we got up as far as Mr. Powells the Baker—some of the colored men says "Let's go and take a drink." We went to the door which was shut, knocked at the door. The colored people used to get drinks there. Mr. Powell did not open the door, but jumped up, came to the window, and shot into the crowd. He hit Isaiah Johnson in the leg, and "little Jacob," of Gen. Lee's plantation in the head; John Proctor in the ankle and Billy Smith in the leg. He shot them with buckshot I believe. I think Powell and his son fired about fifty shots.*
>
> *He fired first. The colored men just let him shoot, the colored men fell back, and after he got done shooting they went back to the house, put fire to it, I don't know who, and began firing into the house at Powell. He fired from the window below. I don't know anything about any colored*

men pushing his wife into the fire. I never heard the colored men threaten anything about going to Powells to attack the house or him.[126]

Wilson believed Feliu's son was present because of the number of rounds fired. However, it was really due to the number of guns Feliu preloaded. As terrifying as this ordeal was, it would not compare to the carnage Wilson would face the next day.

The story of Feliu's death was perhaps the most convoluted story of the entire saga. Newspapers around the country falsely reported that the freedmen murdered numerous others that night, including innocent children and some of Feliu's family members. According to Wilson's testimony, he was aware of a rumor that some of the freedpeople pushed Feliu's wife into the fire. However, Feliu's family was in fact either hiding in the nearby canebrake or in New Orleans at the time. It is unknown whether the newspapers knew the truth of Feliu's family and fabricated information for political or racial motives or they believed the information they published was accurate. The *Columbus Daily Enquirer* based in Columbus, Georgia, reported:

> *The city has all day been filled with rumors of trouble in St. Bernard parish, adjoining New Orleans, below the city. From information brought to headquarters by the sheriff of the parish, and others, it appears that a difficulty occurred yesterday on the occasion of a public display by a couple of Democratic clubs, in which one white man was wounded and two negroes killed, one being a member of the new Metropolitan police force. At night the negroes congregated and proceeded in a body to the house of a Spanish baker, killing him, his son and sister-in-law, and burning his house. His wife escaped with a child in her arms. The other houses reported burned, at one of which four children are reported killed. Rumors are various and conflicting as to the extent of the outrages. Many white inhabitants of the parish deserted their homes last night and fled to this city.*[127]

This article inaccurately speculates that Michael Curtis, the white Metropolitan police officer who was murdered, was African American. Hundreds of newspapers reiterated a similar narrative. The *New York Herald* published this account:

> *Another riot has occurred in Louisiana, and, from the telegraphic accounts, appears to have been attended with more brutal scenes, although with probably the loss of fewer lives, and to have occasioned more deep-seated*

*indignation and excitement among the whites than any of the previous ones.
In St. Bernard parish, just below New Orleans, on Sunday, an affray took
place between negro and white clubs, in which, as usual, the negroes were
the heavier losers in killed and wounded, two of them being killed, while
one white man was wounded. At night, however, the blacks wreaked their
demoniac vengeance on the innocent and helpless, burning three houses and
killing a man and woman, it is believed, five children.*[128]

The article continued with news of "large crowds of white men"
gathering in New Orleans upon hearing the news. They attempted to
charter three steamboats into St. Bernard Parish to join the mayhem but
were refused by General Lovell Harrison Rousseau, who claimed he was
going to send troops to quell the violence. President Andrew Johnson
placed General Rousseau in command of the Department of Louisiana,
a military district encompassing the states of Louisiana and Arkansas.
The *New Orleans Bee*, a bilingual newspaper that published in both French
and English, printed an article titled "Negro Riot in St. Bernard Parish,"
with one subtitle that read, "White Families Massacred or Burned to
Death in Their Houses." The article reported that at least two of Feliu's
children were "certainly" burned alive. On the same night, a distillery
on the Walker Plantation and a coffeehouse were also reported to have
burned to the ground. The article also erroneously claimed that an
elderly white man was killed at the Ducros Railroad Station. The article
sent shockwaves throughout New Orleans with embellished reports that
"the negroes to the number of 1800 or 2000, are burning and killing,
and marching towards the city." Whites near the parish border in New
Orleans mobilized and equipped themselves to enter St. Bernard Parish
at a moment's notice for a preemptive attack. In subsequent paragraphs,
the article stated freedpeople fled the violence and entered New Orleans
"stealthily through the swamps" or others "swam the intervening canals
in their route to the city."[129]

Local newspapers were exceptionally harsh toward the freedpeople. The
Louisiana Democrat relayed this account on November 2:

*The Riot in St. Bernard was started by the negroes who were inflamed
by these speeches and other acts of encouragement from white Radicals.
The Constitution Club of St. Bernard were parading, accompanied by
a delegation from the Seymour Infantes [sic], of this city. One of the
latter Club was insulted by a negro, a few were bantered, when the negro*

drew his pistol and shot the white man, who died soon after. A melee then occurred in which two negroes were killed. Quiet was then restored and everybody supposed the trouble was over. At night the negroes commenced arming at the plantation of Mr. Ong, and soon after surrounded the house of Mr. Pablo Tellio [sic], a baker, a well known Democratic citizen. There were fifty or more of them, and being refused admission, they broke in and immediately murdered Mr. Tellio [sic], a lady relation and three children. Having ransacked the house, set fire to it and burned it. Mrs. Tellio [sic] escaped through a back window. Her husband is said to have fought the fiends desperately, but was overpowered by numbers. The negroes then went to the house of Mr. Manuel Serpas, which they burned, but the family fortunately escaped. The colored man who drove the bread cart for Tellio [sic] was murdered for being a Democrat and another well known Democratic negro, a sugar boiler on the plantation of Olive & Wogan was searched for by the Radical mob and when found he was also murdered. These outrages caused a stampede amongst the residents of the Parish, and they came up [to] the city in vehicles of every kind.[130]

The entire article was fabricated, with the exception of the killing of Feliu, referred to as Mr. Tellio, and the burning of his house. It states that the "Radical mob" murdered a black bread cart driver and a sugar boiler. There is no evidence of either of these killings. Furthermore, it put an unusual amount of blame on the Republican leaders in the parish:

In the Parish of St. Bernard several white men consorting with the negroes, incited them to acts of violence and advised them to commit outrages on the people. Two of these, Mr. Lee, father of General Lee, of the Republican, and Mr. Thos. Ong…have been arrested, both charged with leading and advising the negroes in their lawless conduct. Those who knew Mr. Ong in former years will be surprised to hear, not that he is a Republican, but that he is a Radical of the most bitter type, and is said to have prepared breastworks for the negroes to fight behind, and that on his place their arms and ammunition were stored.…Some of the negroes who have been arrested in St. Bernard Parish state that a white man, whose name has not been ascertained, made them a speech a few days ago, advising them not to care for guns and pistols, but to arm themselves with axes and when the white men were away, they could strike at the root of the family, by making way with the women and children.[131]

The article falsely stated that General Lee and Ong were arrested for inciting the mayhem. Papers supporting the Democrat position reiterated similar stories in both English and French. Some of these stories were most likely designed to conjure up emotions from undecided voters to convince them to vote the Democratic ticket in the upcoming election. Calls for Democrats to vote were accompanied with stories of the "riot." The aforementioned article states, "Democrats! to your posts tomorrow morning bright and early. We repeat it again vote early and then remain on watch all day and do your duty to your party and to your country."[132]

Another version of these rumors reached General Rousseau. He documented them in a report to General Ulysses S. Grant, the highest commanding officer of the U.S. Army and the current presidential candidate. Rousseau wrote:

> From the parish of St. Bernard reports of a highly inflammatory nature were received. A white democratic club in that parish had killed a negro; some citizens had shot a metropolitan policeman. The negroes assembled at night, burnt the house of a leading white democrat and his body with it, drove his wife and little children into the woods, severely beat his sister, and broke the leg of one of his children. These were the facts.[133]

Most coverage skewed facts and constructed falsehoods to support an anti-Republican agenda. The majority of newspapers either favored that perspective or did not question the accuracy of the dominant narrative that the freedpeople escalated the situation. At the end of the bloody Sunday, a number of freedpeople were murdered and two white men, Michael Curtis and Pablo San Feliu, were murdered.

Republican newspapers painted a much different picture of the course of events. The *New Orleans Republican* wrote in its first article concerning the events, "Rumors are rife of trouble in St. Bernard. It is said that yesterday, during the parade of some Democratic clubs, a difficulty arouse and two colored men were killed. Last night the negroes assembled and killed a man named Pablo Felio [*sic*] and burned his house. Great excitement is said to exist."[134]

It then claimed to have a letter from a "planter." The paper did not release the author's name in order to protect the planter, but given the details, it is possible the writer was Thomas Ong, especially considering Ong was a friend of one of the main editors. It read:

We have terrible times in this parish. Murder has been committed on both white [and] black, and add to this the burning of Pablo Felio's [sic] bakery. There is a large gang of armed white men in this parish. I am under guard of one of their own number in my own house. The negroes in this neighborhood have all fled into the woods. Can not some troops be sent into this parish at once? They are wanted here to preserve order. The Sheriff is reported to have fled the parish. General Rousseau has already dispatched troops to the parish, and we feel little doubt but that order will now be preserved. [135]

The murder of Feliu was mentioned in all reports, with Democratic-leaning papers erroneously reporting the additional death of his family members. According to William Hyland, a local historian, Feliu's wife gave a testimony of her version of events. According to her, she went to hide in the canebrake as word of the armed freedmen approached the area. She overheard many freedmen ask Feliu for whiskey, but he refused to sell it to them. The freedmen became agitated and attempted to break into his residence; he responded by lethal force. They eventually broke into his residence and set it ablaze. Feliu was burned alive. Unfortunately, records of her testimony were lost during Hurricane Katrina. [136]

Nonetheless, armed and angry white Democrats had their martyr, regardless of the accuracy of witness testimony. It was the perfect justification needed to intensify the killings. No one slept well that Sunday night. The freedpeople hoped the carnage had ended and federal troops would soon arrive to protect them from any potential dangers. They were gravely mistaken.

Chapter 5

DEVASTATION

This is such a cold bad place I am afraid I will die here.
—Louis Wilson, freedman

The arrival of the troops did not occur as quickly as the freedpeople had anticipated after the chaotic events surrounding Pablo Feliu's murder. At the same time, New Orleans experienced its own racial violence. On Saturday, October 24, predominately white Democratic and predominately black Republican clubs simultaneously held marches and converged on a crowded Canal Street. The Democratic crowd fired into the Republican one, killing seven African Americans. Infuriated by these atrocities, black Republicans went home and armed themselves; they took to the streets in retaliation and killed those they felt attacked them. Federal soldiers temporarily put an end to the violence.[137]

No one died the following day. However, over the course of the subsequent three days, white Democrats patrolled the city; they robbed, looted and killed until federal troops could again restore order. Statistics on the casualties vary from six white citizens and a dozen black citizens murdered to over sixty-three murdered total. The federal troops from the area were preoccupied with establishing order in a bustling New Orleans; St. Bernard Parish was not of priority.[138]

RESIDENTS OF ST. Bernard Parish had to fend for themselves as the spotlight was focused on its populated neighbor. Thomas Ong slept sparingly that Sunday night. By sunrise on Monday morning, October 26, he noticed four armed freedmen sentineled around his plantation. When he inquired about their intentions, the freedmen claimed they had guarded his residence to protect him throughout the night. Ong, appreciative of the help, sent them on their way to avoid conflict.[139]

Angry white residents, with the martyrdom of Feliu as pretext, mobilized to renew hostilities. News of their mobilization spread throughout the parish. Many freedpeople believed the groups were assembling to kill Ong and General A.L. Lee. General Lee was a member of the state legislature and the editor of the *New Orleans Republican*. His unabashed Republican leanings made him a prime target. Freedmen, some armed only with knives and pistols, gathered at General Lee's plantation to protect him. Dr. M.L. Lee, General Lee's father, told them the weapons were unnecessary and not to fire on anyone.[140]

Around nine o'clock in the morning, just as Dr. Lee finished addressing the freedmen, an estimated forty to fifty mounted men with shotguns lined the road in front of General Lee's gate. They were speaking mostly Spanish, but French and Italian were heard as well. Dr. Lee told the freedmen not to panic and that he would personally reason with them to prevent bloodshed. The freedmen warned him that the mob would not reason with him; instead, they would kill him.[141]

Dr. Lee was unfazed by their warnings. Dr. Lee had practiced medicine before venturing into the political arena in the 1840s. In 1859, he was elected to the U.S. Congress as a Republican. He was an educated doctor, a politician and believed himself to be a skilled negotiator. The experienced sixty-three-year-old mounted his horse and rode toward the men while waving a white handkerchief as a gesture of peace. Adolph Jones, a freedman who spoke multiple languages, accompanied him in case translation was needed. As they approached the group, the men cocked and aimed their shotguns at him. Dr. Lee waved his handkerchief harder to ensure he meant no harm. The men ignored his gesture, swiftly surrounded Dr. Lee and Jones, knocked Dr. Lee off his horse and apprehended him and Jones. Dr. Lee was stunned that he was not provided a chance to negotiate. They then turned their guns toward the freedmen and fired a barrage of bullets. The freedmen dispersed into the cane fields to escape.[142]

Lieutenant J.M. Lee visited General Lee's plantation during his investigation with the Freedmen's Bureau. He received this account from Adolph Jones:

> *The Doctor went up waving his white handkerchief, and they, the Spanish, had their guns pointed towards us as though they intended shooting us. We went on top to them. They were coming on towards us in line. They arrested the Dr. and myself—David Jones, Leone Porter, Antonio Campo. These were the ones that arrested us in particular. They stopped us, took us in charge. All of them wanted us there. They spoke so, because I understood them, as I speak Spanish and understand French, and know the most of them. I know what they meant by their language. All of them said "Kill the Doctor, that it was him and General—General Lee—that was causing the trouble in the country." They not only spoke it among themselves but said so to the Doctor.*
>
> *They said—that is Tremier and others—I know all of them—that they would kill the Dr.—"they would not shoot him down but would take him to the house, and make him pull off his shoes, and pull the trigger of a shot gun with his toe and shoot himself that way." They did not speak this in English, but said so in French, and I knew what they said.*
>
> *The Dr. and myself were taken to the house—the Coffee House (Manuel Flores) and they all wanted to know of me what the Doctor come up there for, that is to the gate, I told them he came for peace, to prevent bloodshed, but they do not believe it so, but I repeatedly told them and kept talking to them that way,—that the Dr. had not come for any other purpose than peace hoping that they would believe me far enough to keep them from killing the Dr.*[143]

The men seemed intent on killing Dr. Lee despite the pleas from Jones, but they did not feel it was sensible to kill him in the open road, especially considering he was the father of a renowned Union general. Many poor whites viewed Dr. Lee and his son, General Lee, as carpetbaggers who moved down to capitalize on their downtrodden economy after the Civil War. Local whites had little sympathy for them. Jones and other freedmen spoke fluent Spanish and translated the excited words of the captors to Dr. Lee. Dr. Lee and the freedpeople were transported to Florey's Coffeehouse, a local coffee shop converted into a makeshift prison. Dr. Lee and dozens of freedpeople, including Louis Wilson, were held captive.[144]

THROUGHOUT THE ENTIRE day, meandering vigilantes, many masquerading as police, roamed and killed freedpeople. They raided all the ex-slave quarters, still inhabited by freedpeople, to steal what they could appropriate for personal use and, most importantly, destroy registration papers. They were determined to return the parish to a Democratic stronghold by instilling terror and fear into the hearts of the freedpeople.[145]

According to the 1869 report by the Louisiana General Assembly, "It was dangerous for a colored or white Republican to walk the street by day or night. The marauders…sacked houses, robbed the people of money, moveables, arms and registration papers; killed men and hacked them to pieces with bowie knives, and prevented the civil officers from performing their functions."[146]

Notable white Republicans were prime targets for angry Democrats. A group of thirty armed white men visited Judge A.G. Thornton's residence the same morning. They broke into his home and stole numerous articles. In one of Judge Thornton's testimonies, he claimed that they took his

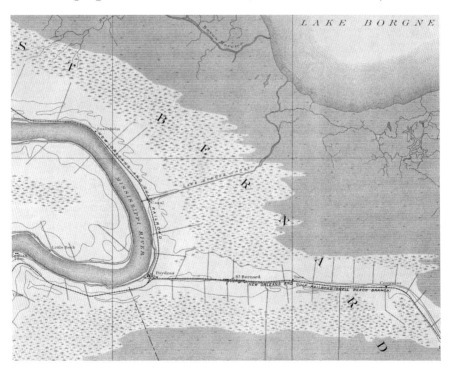

A U.S. Geological Survey map of lower St. Bernard Parish showing the area from the Mississippi River to the Bayou Terre-aux-Boeufs region. The massacre took place within this vicinity. *U.S. Geological Survey.*

"hat, two guns, table-knives, carving knives, and many sundry household articles." They also flipped his mattress and, "in one case, making three little sick children get up" to "search between the mattresses…for money or silverware." The ransacking of Judge Thornton's home demonstrated a disregard for the law by the assailants because they did not fear getting caught or prosecuted. They acted with impunity.[147]

At a similar time that the events occurred at Dr. Lee's plantation and Judge Thornton's residence, a group of about fifteen to twenty white men, headed by Vallvey Veillon, went to the old slave quarters at the Davis and Millaudon Plantations. There, they shot indiscriminately as freedpeople scurried into the cane fields for safety. One of them was shot during the mayhem. The group then plundered the empty cabins and stole guns, cooking knives, canes, money, clothing and marriage and registration papers. The freedmen could not vote in the upcoming presidential election without registration papers.[148]

J.M. Lee recorded the account of Felis Thomas, a freedwoman, who was present during the raid:

> On Monday the 26th of Oct., 1868 about 8 o'clock in the morning, they came in here to this place, the Spanish, about twenty of them. Three or four of them came in with shot guns hallowing. I ran from them when I saw them coming because I was afraid they were going to shoot me. Ran about a hundred yards, they were shooting at me, and hit me with a shot near my house. I was trying to get to my house. They shot me in the left leg below the knee, I fell down, they came up to me. I got up and walked into my house, they came in behind me. Mr. Alma Marshall, he shot me with a shot gun, was on his horse when he shot me. Vellvey Veillon was the head man with the twenty white men.
>
> Alma Marshall and another white man came into my house—took my husband's gun and pistol, powder, horn and flash, shot and caps. They then went for my brother—William Boss. They searched his house, took his gun, powder, and shot and a walking cane of his, and his pistol. My brother tried to run away from them, but they shot at him, and shot a hole through his clothes—back of his coat—He had to run away to save his life—I know most of the men who were with the party of Vellvey Veillon.[149]

Later in the afternoon, a different group of white men, led by Confederate veteran Victor Estopinal, a younger cousin of Albert Estopinal, went to the cabins of the freedpeople at the Dar Quan Plantation. They murdered one freedman and shot three others. Another group headed to Marrero's plantation. An elderly freedman around ninety years of age identified as "Nelson" was shot to death. The parties plundered the plantations in a similar fashion to Veillon's posse, with registration papers being the top priority of the raids.[150]

A few hours later, different armed men led by a man masquerading as sheriff, identified only as Le Blanc in documents, assembled in front of Ong's plantation. They yelled for him to exit his domicile because he was under arrest. Ong knew the men were not authorized police and refused to leave his boarded-up residence.[151]

A freedman who worked for Ong happened on the group by accident as he was returning from New Orleans with fifteen dollars' worth of purchases. The man was unaware of the ongoing carnage. Seeing his valuables, the group shot at him. He dropped his goods and ran. He was caught by one of his assailants but escaped into the cane fields before facing his demise.[152]

It was not until the arrival of Brevet Major Kinzie Bates with another contingent of U.S. federal troops from Jackson Barracks that the vigilantes had to continue their killing in a more covert manner. Upon arrival at the courthouse, he received a message from Ong. According to Bates's testimony:

> While there I received a message from Mr. Thomas Ong, living about two miles distant, requesting me to come to his place, as his life was in danger. I placed eight men in a wagon and directed the balance of my company to follow me on foot. As I approached his place I noticed about a dozen white men, armed, sitting in front of his gate. As I reached the gate about sixty mounted men, armed with double-barreled shot-guns, came up. They had some freedman prisoners. Mr. Ong came out and placed himself under my protection. I asked this party what their object was. I was informed they were a sheriff's posse, who were arresting the supposed murderers of Pablo Fileo [sic]. Le Blanc, the deputy sheriff, came up and spoke to me. I asked him at once to disperse his posse; that I would take care of the parish. They marched over to the court-house with their prisoners, and I saw no more of them. There was a very little feeling existing amongst these people against Mr. Ong.[153]

The timely arrival of Major Bates probably saved Ong's life, since the "posse" blamed Ong for inciting the freedmen to murder Feliu. Dozens of freedpeople descended on Ong's residence once word of Major Bates's arrival spread in hope of protection. The saga would have ended differently had Major Bates not arrived. Although many were joyful for his arrival, he had specific orders not to intervene with the ongoing violence "unless called upon to do so by the civil authorities." However, the proper civil authorities no longer wielded power.[154]

At approximately 2:00 p.m., a bipartisan meeting consisting of Governor Warmoth, General A.L. Lee and other prominent Democrats and Republicans met in New Orleans to call General Lovell Harrison Rousseau for immediate assistance to quell the troubles in St. Bernard Parish. General Rousseau was a Democrat from Kentucky, a decorated Union veteran and a skilled negotiator who had assisted with the purchase of Alaska from Russia a year prior. He quickly dispatched messages to Secretary of War John Schofield and President Andrew Johnson for advice. The leaders of the New Orleans meeting sent out a proclamation "requesting no public meetings or processions by either political party before the balloting." The proclamation was either ignored or went unnoticed by Democratic clubs.[155]

MEANWHILE, AT FLOREY'S coffee shop, where Dr. Lee, Louis Wilson, Adolph Jones and others were held captive, the horror started. As the sun disappeared beyond the swamp, the mob found it safer to execute their victims. Dr. Lee witnessed four freedmen, including Louis Wilson, taken outside by some of the armed men who had kidnapped him. He heard several gunshots, and the armed men returned without the freedmen. Wilson survived the execution and gave his testimony to Lieutenant J.M. Lee: "When I was coming back from the Court House, they took me up at Frejus place, some white men did. Mr. Warren Cheek, is the head man,—Moassis—white men made me get down off my horse. He struck me with the gun he had, on my jaw. They then took me down to Florey's about sunset."[156]

He continued that men, whom he knew and could identify, took him and others outside. He described the execution:

> I don't know whether these men fired on me, but I think they fired on the rest of them. When they fired on me they broke off and ran. I got into some weed and I laid down, that is the time some one came up and shot me in the shoulder, (supposed to be Leone Pato). When they went away I crawled a little farther,—staid [sic] out all that night,—the next day. I staied [sic] three days in the woods. I got strength a little and I came home. That's all I know. I am wounded in six places. On the shoulder, in my legs and in one foot. This is such a cold bad place I am afraid I will die here. I want to be taken to a hospital.[157]

ADOLPH JONES, THE other freedman held captive at Florey's, claimed in his testimony that he witnessed Wilson and others being taken out back. He then heard about "twelve" shots. Only one of the freedmen returned. For unknown reasons, he was removed from the execution and spared. When the spared freedman returned to Florey's, he told Jones and the others of the execution. The freedman warned Jones and others not to repeat what had happened lest they suffer a similar fate.[158]

Major Bates and General Lee heard of these horrors and sent a force to release the freedpeople and Dr. Lee. General Lee rescued his father, Dr. Lee, and escorted him to Ong's plantation. Ong and Dr. Lee were escorted by federal troops to a safe haven in New Orleans. Ong met with General Rousseau to discuss the events. Ong ate and slept better that night. The freedpeople of St. Bernard Parish were not granted that same luxury. The horror for them continued:

> *For the succeeding three days bodies of armed white men, notwithstanding the presence of United States troops who were there to aid the civil authorities in preserving peace, prowled around the parish killing and maltreating every colored man that appeared on the road, and not content with this went to their residences, robbed them of their money, provisions, clothing, registration-papers, and in some instances the discharge-papers of discharged soldiers were taken.*[159]

Chapter 6

RAMIFICATION

You son of a bitch if you move I'll kill you.
—armed man to a freedman

The arrival of federal troops had a slight impact on the violence. It prompted Sheriff Chalaire, the legitimate sheriff, to act, perhaps because he felt safe in doing so or because he felt legally obligated. Indiscriminate slaughter was no longer a viable option for the armed pillaging groups.[160]

President Andrew Johnson gave General Lovell Rousseau full authority to subdue the violence surrounding the presidential election. On October 31, President Johnson replied to General Rousseau:

> *You are expected and authorized to take all legitimate steps necessary and proper to prevent breaches of the peace or hostile collisions between citizens. Questions relating to the civil polity of the State must be left to the proper civil authorities for consideration and settlement. The object is to preserve peace and restore civil Government to the people according to the principles laid down in the Constitution.*
>
> *You are referred to the instructions heretofore given, which are deemed full and ample for all just and law purposes.*[161]

Despite a deceleration, the killings did not cease. Vallvey Veillon returned to the Millaudon Plantation. Jane Ackus, a freedwoman who survived her first encounter without being shot, was seeking safety in her cabin when

Veillon arrived. He went into her house and drew his pistol. Ackus claimed in her testimony that he shot her in her "heart three times." She cried, "For God's sake don't, I have not done you any thing at all!" She barely survived the attack.[162]

On Sunday, November 1, men masquerading as the police appeared at a smaller plantation where Eugene Joseph was working that evening. The men sent a younger teenager, identified by Joseph as Yono, to confront Joseph. Joseph described the incident to Lieutenant J.M. Lee:

> Then he [Yono] jumped on me and struck me in the face with his fists holding my collar, and he pulled out his knife and wanted to stab me, and I ran from him and he struck at me with his knife. I dodged and the knife just struck in my shirt, right here where you see my shirt open, and they run behind me on horse back, and then they shot me in the right breast, the ball lodged in my left side and is still in there. I don't know the full name of the boy who struck at me with the knife, but Serapis Youa shot me with a revolver, I fell down and could not move, turned my head to look around and he came right on me…and he said "you son of a bitch if you move I'll kill you."[163]

Joseph later states in his testimony that the man who shot him bragged, "This is the way you put a ball through a d----d nigger." (It's interesting to note that J.M. Lee did not spell out certain expletives but kept the racial pejorative intact throughout his investigation.) After the incident, they arrested Joseph and brought him to the courthouse in hidden view of the nearby federal troops. J.M. Lee noted the frequency with which freedpeople were "shot first and arrested afterward." Judge A.G. Thornton, also an experienced physician, saw Joseph twice to address his wounds, and Joseph attributed his recovery to these visits. Despite this treatment, Joseph bore the scars of this ordeal throughout his life. Even as he testified against his attackers, the bullet remained lodged in his chest.[164]

On November 3, a freedman identified only as Arnold started the morning early with his wife to dig and plant potatoes. In the distance, they noticed the hazy silhouettes of six armed men approaching in their direction. Arnold's wife, having heard of stories of outbreaks and violence nearby, knew nothing positive could emerge from staying put and attempting to reason with these men. She urged her husband to get out of sight and "hide in the cane." Arnold argued that he had committed no crime and thus had no reason to hide. If he told the approaching men what they wanted to hear, Arnold was sure they would move along. His wife, believing otherwise, fled to the fields. J.M. Lee documented the story of Arnold's wife: "His wife hid in the cane and she heard the men as they came up, ask her husband if he had voted, and what ticket he voted. He said he had voted the Democratic ticket, and then they told him to go along with them and they would see if it was so, and after going afew [*sic*] steps his wife heard him exclaim, 'Oh pray Master.'"[165]

His body was found stabbed in six places and dismembered. The coroner claimed he "came to his death by being stabbed by some unknown parties." The unmitigated violence of the act speaks to the mindset of these men. The killers wanted Arnold to feel pain as opposed to the quick death a bullet could provide; they were willing to expend extra effort on their part to inflict it.[166]

There were many reported cases in which the killers sought to maximize suffering of the victims even at the expense of their own time and energy. In one case, a young freedman was abducted and "cut all to pieces in a horrible manner" with a bowie knife because he would not "hurrah for Seymour and Blair." Similarly, a freedwoman was "shot in the abdomen" and left to die in a "gutter pleading for mercy." Both of these instances occurred in proximity to the parish courthouse in a clear demonstration that the law was of no concern to the perpetrators.[167]

The killings did subside, at least openly, with the presence of federal troops. Governor Henry C. Warmoth's request to General Lovell Rousseau for additional assistance to ensure a safe election was denied. It is uncertain why Rousseau denied the request. At best, he might have felt the move was unnecessary or that he did not have the manpower. At worst, he might not have been concerned with protecting the freedpeople. Regardless, Warmoth realized St. Bernard Parish was a lost cause for the Republican Party despite having a clear majority with approximately seven hundred registered Republicans. He issued a public statement requesting freedmen to avoid the polls in St. Bernard Parish and other volatile regions, as safety could not be guaranteed.[168]

The political ramifications were dire. Every supervisor of registration authorized to conduct the election was jailed, murdered or fled. As a result, the sheriff supervised the election instead. Ulysses S. Grant received only one vote from St. Bernard Parish despite the parish having recently voted in a Republican judge, a Republican governor and a Republican constitution and having a Republican majority. All but one Republican running the elections received a single vote; the remaining Republican candidate got two. Except for one brave entity, black and white Republicans alike avoided the voting booths. The Democrats' reign of terror succeeded in sealing a Seymour victory for the parish and throughout Louisiana. However, upon further investigation on the legality of the election in the parish, considering it was administered by the sheriff as opposed to legitimate supervisors, the federal government rendered the parish vote invalid. Overall, Grant won the nation due to the black vote, becoming the first president to win with a minority of the white vote. According to historian John C. Rodrigue, "Republicans captured the presidency in 1868, but white terror carried the day in Louisiana."[169]

Even though the election was over and the federal troops occupied the parish, armed men still patrolled the roads at night. It was unsafe for any known white Republican or person of color to travel. On November 15, John Lewis Spalding, the commanding officer of the federal troops in St. Bernard Parish, was traveling alone in lower St. Bernard Parish. He stopped at Thomas Ong's plantation to change his tired horse for a mule. He described the night as "exceedingly dark." When Spalding was on the "most lonesome part of the road," he heard someone cry "halt" to his mule. The mule stopped in its tracks. Spalding demanded to know the cause of halt and drew his pistol from inside the carriage to prepare for a duel. An armed man on horseback put his lantern close to the carriage to see who was inside. Spalding could see silhouettes of more armed mounted men approaching his carriage. Spalding announced he was the commanding officer of federal troops and heard a voice translate his announcement in Spanish. The person who translated rode up to the carriage and claimed he was attempting to frighten a friend. They retreated back into the darkness. Spalding believed they may have thought he was Ong or General A.L. Lee since he had borrowed their mule and carriage, respectively. The men most likely did not attack Spalding in fear of the inevitable retaliation from U.S. troops. Had it been a different Republican, or a freedperson, the outcome would unequivocally have been much more grim.[170]

WHITE DEMOCRATS WERE infuriated knowing the killers of Pablo Feliu had not been forced to answer for their actions. Judge Thornton, the elected judge of the parish, was powerless to act; his authority was no longer respected due to his political leanings. He claimed in his testimony, "I will here state that it is impossible for me to act as parish judge for this parish, either in civil or in criminal cases. Neither parish officers or witnesses pay any attention to my official orders. Furthermore, I will say that I am the only officer in the parish of Saint Bernard who has taken the oath of eligibility."[171]

He noted that the parish had "no police-jury," even though Governor Warmoth himself had appointed one with "six magistrates" and "six constables and an assessor" six weeks prior to the election. A police jury is a legislative and executive governing body typical of older Louisiana parishes that is essential to maintaining order. When asked, Thornton claimed that "most of the police-jury have been murdered, and every one of the rest of the appointees have been frightened away by being charged in some way or other in producing the riots."[172]

Due to the ineptness of Judge Thornton, a local autocrat took measures into his own hands. Philippe Toca, known for his harshness, styled himself as the judge of the parish despite not having been elected and having no legitimate claim to the title. He once challenged Judge Gilbert Leonard of neighboring Plaquemines Parish to a duel where the two exchanged blows with double-barreled fowling pieces fifty yards apart. Judge Leonard did not survive. After the duel, few questioned Toca's legal validity. Freedpeople felt his wrath after the massacre.

Toca gathered a posse and visited plantations throughout the parish and arrested indiscriminately. Within a matter of days, he had arrested an estimated sixty-four freedpeople and charged them with the killing of Feliu. Toca only released individuals who could buy their freedom. He charged some of the arrested upward of nine dollars, almost a month's salary. Officer Zuinglius McKay was tasked to investigate the arrests and subsequent extreme interrogations unlawfully carried out by Toca. He remarked:

He [Toca] *proceeded to issue warrants, and by some parties unauthorized to make arrests, and carried before this would-be justice of the peace. They were all put in jail. No distinction was made between them, whether they were witnesses or not; they were all placed in jail, charged with the murder of Pablo Feilio* [sic]. *Then commenced a system of examination and interrogation unknown before to any other government with a free constitution, and only equaled by the terrors of the Spanish inquisition, a few centuries back, or the later cruelties practiced by King Bomba, of Naples, previous to his overthrow by the Italian government. The parties were forced to make voluntary confessions, and strong endeavors were made to compel the parties giving testimony to implicate innocent parties. Witnesses dare not state facts, as they were surrounded by armed cut-throats and murderers.*[173]

After the interrogations, the self-styled Judge Toca unilaterality declared all the suspects guilty and transported them to the parish prison in New Orleans on November 11. According to J.M. Lee's investigation, the freedpeople received "barbarous" treatment while detained. A prisoner named Sam Bucks and his associates immediately made their supremacy known to the newcomers and relentlessly attacked the freedpeople from St. Bernard Parish.[174]

On November 20, a writ of habeas corpus was sued on behalf of the freedpeople by Republican sympathizers. The accused were presented to Judge Edmund Abell to have their case heard. Judge Abell was a Union supporter but was also known for his proslavery perspective. He once remarked, "I say that of all systems of labor, slavery is the most perfect, humane, and satisfactory that has ever been devised; and a slave under a good master is the most happy being in the world." Despite his views regarding slavery, Judge Abell immediately dismissed the authority of Philippe Toca, and all the detainees were considered innocent of their suspected crimes. Most of the freedpeople were released and immediately returned to St. Bernard Parish to work on the plantations. However, the judge held those whom he believed were directly involved for six to seven months without trial before he released them.[175]

Toca was appalled by the decision of Judge Abell and immediately rearrested the freedpeople. J.M. Lee wrote a letter to Judge Thornton to give orders to stop the illegal arrests:

I am informed that steps are being taken by the so-called civil authorities of this parish to arrest the second time a certain freedmen recently released upon a hearing before proper civil authority in the city of New Orleans, viz: Sixty-four (64) freed people, more or less, who were arraigned before on Judge Toca, charged with participating in the troubles which occurred in this parish on or about the 25th day of October, 1868, and who were sent to the city to be confined, at the instance or by the pretended authority of the said Judge Toca, and which freed people were released by competent civil authority in the said city of New Orleans.

Now as you have taken measures for the re-arrest of these parties or some of them, without knowing the full facts attending their release, and as it is well known that civil authority is disorganized and inoperative in this parish, and that the re-arrest and trial of these freedmen in the manner indicated will be neither just nor impartial, you are hereby informed, by direction of Brevet Major-General Hatch, assistant commissioner, that no such arrests will be allowed upon these freedmen, who have gone peaceably to work on the plantations where they were employed, and any steps taken by you in that direction will be stopped.

You are also notified that if necessary to prevent such premature proceedings, the freedmen referred to will be at once taken under charge of and the Bureau of R., F. and A. Lands of this State, and will be held for trial and produced when required before any civil court having proper jurisdiction, which can proceed in their cases without intimidation.[176]

Toca abandoned his charade as a legitimate judge to avoid the perceived infiltration of more federal troops. Instead, he threatened and intimidated Judge Thornton himself to issue warrants for the arrests of the freedpeople. Under duress, Thornton acquiesced and issued warrants to arrest certain freedpeople. Once the warrants were issued, Toca and his de facto police force took it upon themselves to adhere to the orders, a vastly different response to Thornton than the previous months. Nothing seemed to come from these arrests, as Thornton noted the arrests were a farce and released most of those detained. Over sixty freedpeople were arrested and held for months for the murder of one white person. By contrast, in the murders and attempted murders of multiple freedpeople, cases in which many of the survivors could identify their attackers, not a single white assailant was once questioned or detained. When J.M. Lee was conducting his investigation, he "requested a number of whites to give…information," but "they pretended to know but little about it."[177]

THE OVERALL DEATH toll of the tragedy is impossible to accurately determine. Lieutenant J.M. Lee noted in the conclusion of his report that nine freedpersons were killed and seventeen were wounded, while two whites were killed and one wounded. However, Lee mentions more than nine freedpeople killed throughout his investigation. Lee states in the beginning of his report, "The principal casualties have been given, but there are many of a minor character that have not been reported." It's important to note that he only gathered testimonies of eleven freedpeople out of over two thousand living in the parish. He also did not stay in the parish long enough to conduct a full investigation, probably due to fear, as the perpetrators were not fond of any inquiries into the violent affair. Furthermore, he added a note at the bottom of his report: "The above embraces all casualties as far as ascertained, but I am of the opinion that there are others not yet made known."[178]

Judge Thornton provided a more gruesome figure in his testimony. He claimed, "I do not mean to say that there were only (35) thirty-five negroes who were murdered during the riots. I have no doubt there were many more, but these were all that were officially reported to me." Thornton discussed other murders not mentioned by Lee, most notably the fact that some of the police jury members were murdered.[179]

Others in addition to Thornton contributed to the growing number of lives of freedpeople lost in the massacre. Philip Taylor, a Metropolitan policeman, claimed "there were from thirty-five to fifty colored people killed" during the mayhem. Taylor also revealed different murders not previously discussed. Major Bates claimed that there were two white men who were killed, Michael Curtis and Pablo Feliu; in regard to freedpeople, however, he asserted it was "impossible to find out the exact number of killed, as many of the freedmen were hid in the cane." Bates claimed the majority of freedmen would not converse with him because they "were evidently under the impression that they would be marked and suffer bodily harm."[180]

The aforementioned 1869 report by the Louisiana General Assembly put the fatalities at an even higher estimate: "The total number of killed during this massacre which were counted was thirty-eight (38). The number killed, of whom reliable information was received was sixty-eight (68). It is probable that many men were killed in the swamps and other secret places, whose number is known only to the murderers and to God."[181]

A United States Congress Joint Select Committee tasked with investigating "insurrectionary states" referenced the 68 figure in its report. An 1875 investigation by the U.S. House of Representatives claimed that the "atrocities committed in Saint Bernard Parish" resulted in the "slaughter of 135 colored" persons. While this estimate is not explicitly corroborated by other accounts, the report does detail some deaths not mentioned in other findings: "Colored women had their breasts cut off, and when in a condition of pregnancy were literally ripped open." The report also reveals how a massacre in rural southeast Louisiana was so severe that it provoked a response from then president Andrew Johnson. President Johnson was forced to release certain U.S. Army officers from duty due to their failures to stop the mayhem in St. Bernard Parish. Overall, the evidence at the time collectively suggests at least 35 victims. Unfortunately, the exact death toll will never be adequately determined, given the chaos generated by the violence.[182]

Chapter 7

DECONSTRUCTION

What remains certain is that Reconstruction failed, and that for blacks its failure was a disaster whose magnitude cannot be obscured by the genuine accomplishments that did endure.
—*historian Eric Foner,* Reconstruction: America's Unfinished Revolution

The population of St. Bernard Parish decreased drastically in the 1860s and experienced its first significant decline since its establishment. In 1860, the population was at 4,076. By 1870, it had dwindled to 3,553. The white population declined approximately 7 percent, while the black population declined approximately 17 percent. The overall 12.8 percent decrease was the largest in St. Bernard Parish history until Hurricane Katrina in 2005. Freedpeople looked for emerging opportunities elsewhere, most notably in New Orleans, which saw its black population double during the same decade.[183]

The political, economic and social ramifications of the Civil War; the start of Reconstruction; and the violence in 1868 were profound on the character of St. Bernard Parish. Impoverished ethnic groups who had lived in relative peace for almost a century turned violent. Neighbors attacked neighbors; friends attacked friends. Many of the surviving victims knew the aggressors personally. The identity of the region shifted, and its aftermath was felt during the continuation of Reconstruction and the subsequent Bourbon Era.

Reconstruction in Louisiana was a tumultuous era. The violence the freedpeople experienced in St. Bernard Parish in 1868 was felt in other regions in Louisiana, perhaps at more alarming rates. In St. Landry Parish, the Seymour Knights and the Knights of the White Camellia, white supremacist organizations, pursued "their victims through the swamps and forests" and killed freedpeople indiscriminately for three gruesome days before the 1868 presidential election. At least 150 were murdered. Around Shreveport, in Bossier and Caddo Parishes, armed mobs committed similar crimes. Witnesses testified of seeing dozens of bodies floating down the Red River. Fatalities are estimated around 200. The Republican registered vote in Caddo Parish was 2,894; Ulysses S. Grant received 1 vote. The Republican registered vote in neighboring Bossier Parish was 1,938; Grant also received 1 vote.[184]

The carnage was statewide. State officials attempting to ascertain the fatalities in 1868 reported 784 freedpeople murdered and 450 wounded. A subsequent federal report estimated the number killed at over 1,000. The terror succeeded in its goal of voter suppression. In July, Republican Warmoth received 65,000 votes in seeking his governorship. In November, Republican Grant received a mere 33,225 votes across the state, slightly more than half of Warmoth. Grant did not receive a solitary vote in seven parishes.[185]

Although Reconstruction was a challenging time for African Americans, many had more clout than the days of slavery during the antebellum era. Many exercised their newly acquired rights to demand higher wages and better treatment when their labor was most desired. Many planters outsourced their work to immigrants in order to combat such unrest and undermine the growing leverage of black laborers. In 1864, the federal government legalized the *padrone* system, which allowed the aggressive and oftentimes dishonest recruitment of immigrants under misleading contracts. Incoming Italians, chiefly Sicilians, signed these contracts in hopes of employment and better economic opportunities. Planters exploited these incoming Italians who were contractually obligated to work long hours for miniscule pay.[186]

Europeans were not the only ones lured by the promise of economic opportunities. Starting in 1867, Chinese laborers were also recruited to work the plantations in southeast Louisiana. By 1870, over 1,600 Chinese workers had been recruited from areas ranging from California to mainland China. This newfound competition between laborers stunted the negotiating power of black laborers.[187]

At the Millaudon Plantation, 140 Chinese laborers were recruited in 1870 to work a three-year contract. They were to be paid "fourteen dollars in gold per month" along with "daily rations of fresh meat, rice, and tea." Upon arrival, the Chinese laborers noticed their black counterparts leaving around noon on Saturdays to enjoy their long afternoon while they continued to toil the crops. The Chinese laborers demanded the same, but the planter would not acquiesce. They demanded the planter pay for their vegetables. The planter paid but told them "to expect no more." They then requested ten acres of land to grow and sell their own vegetables, but the request was denied. Cum Wing, a San Francisco contractor who negotiated their contracts, was kidnapped by the laborers during one of his routine visits to the worksite. The Metropolitan Police were called to rescue Wing and arrested 14 ringleaders. Shortly after, the Chinese laborers attacked the overseer, who returned fire. The entire workforce bombarded the overseer, causing him to run. He never returned back to work. Out of the 140 Chinese laborers recruited to work for three years, 115 abandoned their positions within fourteen months.[188]

That same year, a journalist from the *New Orleans Republic* visited the Millaudon Plantation to analyze the relations between the "colored" laborers and their "new competition." There seemed to be no rivalry between them. One woman of color, "old auntie," said the new workers were friendly and "don't do nuffin to nobody; mind der own bisness." Others reiterated similar sentiments. The article concluded that there was no "feeling of jealousy among the colored folks in the neighborhood of the Chinese" and there was "good feeling between them."[189]

THE 1870s WAS another violent decade for freedpeople in Louisiana. In 1872, Republican William Pitt Kellogg won the governorship despite Democrats winning large gains at other levels of government. The election was heavily disputed, and both Kellogg and John McEnery, the Democratic candidate, held inauguration parties to celebrate their victory. The federal government backed Kellogg; the backlash to a Republican governor was severe.

In 1873, racial tensions escalated in Colfax, Grant Parish. In 1869, Colfax was named after vice presidential candidate Schuyler M. Colfax, and Grant Parish was named after Ulysses S. Grant. Many freedpeople in the area gathered in Colfax for protection as violence erupted. On April 5, 1873, an unarmed black farmer was shot through the head by a white man, which launched the region into chaos that resembled St. Bernard Parish in 1868.[190] The majority of freedpeople surrendered after dozens were murdered by the marauding groups. At least 48 freedpeople were killed after being held in custody for the afternoon. The total fatality count is disputed because many victims were tossed into the river. Conservative estimates put the death toll around 60, while other estimates reach upward of 150. In a similar fashion to the massacre in St. Bernard Parish, the events were dubbed the "Colfax Riot" by Democrat-leaning newspapers, and "massacre" was applied by black-owned newspapers or newspapers with Republican leanings or sympathies. The perpetrators of the Colfax Massacre and their sympathizers organized the White League, a paramilitary group committed to violence to end Reconstruction. Paramilitary groups took note of these successes and joined the White League or organized similar groups throughout Louisiana. The White League recruited statewide and morphed into a quasi-army.[191]

The case to prosecute the perpetrators in Grant Parish led to the *United States v. Cruikshank et al* Supreme Court case. The landmark decision undermined legislation that granted the federal government the authority to

Freedpeople hiding in the swamps to escape violence. *Harper's Weekly*, 1873. *Courtesy of the Library of Congress.*

A member of the White League shakes hands with a KKK member over an African American couple holding a deceased baby. An African American hangs from a tree in the background. *Harper's Weekly*, 1874. *Courtesy of the Library of Congress.*

impose Reconstruction in the South. The Enforcement Act of 1870, which was enacted to prosecute paramilitary organizations similar to the White League, was nullified. It was a fatal blow for freedpeople in St. Bernard Parish and throughout Louisiana. The success of staunch anti-Republicans at Colfax ignited a new spark for overthrowing Republican rule via black disenfranchisement.

In August 1874, in Coushatta Parish, the White League kidnapped six Republican officeholders and a few of their family members and rounded up twenty-five nearby freedpeople. They coerced the officeholders to sign a document stating they would leave the region. They were executed before that chance was granted to them. The freedpeople were killed because they witnessed the atrocity. No members of the White League were charged.

A month later, McEnery and his loyal supporters organized a legislature in New Orleans and orchestrated a coup to oust Kellogg. The legislature mobilized the White League, including members from St. Bernard Parish, to provide over 5,000 armed militants, many of them ex-Confederates, as a de facto army. The Metropolitan Police and the state militia, which included both African Americans and ex-Confederates, were tasked to defend the city with a smaller force of approximately 3,500. On September 14, 1874, a usually bustling Canal Street of commerce was turned into a bloody battleground. James Longstreet, a former Confederate general and Metropolitan officer, attempted to halt the violence of the White League. He was shot and taken prisoner. The conflict, dubbed the Battle of Liberty Place, resulted in an estimated over 100 causalities and a decisive victory by the White League.[192]

The new government occupied government buildings, inaugurated McEnery and exercised control of the entire city for three days. President Grant sent federal troops to restore order; the White League retreated prior to their arrival. As with many other violent episodes during Reconstruction, no arrests were made. Although the Battle of Liberty Place did not achieve the desired results for the White League and Democrats, it sent shockwaves throughout St. Bernard Parish and the entire region. The Metropolitan Police and state militias were disrupted beyond repair. Kellogg maintained his power through force by federal troops, but his authority was almost nonexistent in rural Louisiana. The White League increased its influence in New Orleans, St. Bernard Parish and throughout Louisiana.[193]

In 1876, Democrats regained control of the state legislature. In the same year, Democrat Francis T. Nicholls won the gubernatorial election. The majority of the White League morphed into the state militia and the National Guard. Supporters of Nicholls marched on the Cabildo, the Louisiana Supreme Court, and ousted the Supreme Court justices. Nicholls then appointed justices who would appease white supremacists. Nationally, the disputed 1876 U.S. presidential election was settled through an agreement that federal troops would be removed from the South if the South conceded to a victory for Republican Rutherford B. Hayes. The Compromise of 1877 officially ended Reconstruction in the South.[194]

The end of Reconstruction meant the black population in St. Bernard Parish would not have the level of protection granted under federal occupation. Voter records show that voter intimidation increased after 1877. When Democrat Nicholls ran for governor in 1876, he received 48.4 percent of the St. Bernard Parish vote, demonstrating a significant black voter turnout. However, when Democrat Louis A. Wiltz ran for governor after Reconstruction ended, he won 65.5 percent of the parish vote despite the notion that the majority of the voter eligible population was black. The pattern was similar across local, state and federal elections.[195]

BOURBON ERA

After federal occupation ceased, Louisiana entered the Bourbon Era, a reactionary period dating from the Louisiana Constitution of 1879 until the Constitution of 1898. Its name derives from the Bourbon kings who dominated the political landscape in France after the fall of Napoleon Bonaparte. The Bourbon kings sought to reverse the monumental political and economic gains provided by the French Revolution. They favored archaic laws designed to reestablish royal power at the expense of France's middle and lower classes. Like the Bourbon kings of France, the Bourbon Democrats of Louisiana sought to restore policies that favored the elites and reverse gains made during Reconstruction. Once they obtained power, the impact was immediate for St. Bernard Parish.

The quality of life for black citizens during the Bourbon Era worsened in St. Bernard Parish and throughout Louisiana. They were left unprotected and vulnerable. The quality of life for whites did not improve either. The lower class suffered from economic and social immobility. Bourbon Democrats saw and seized the opportunity to exploit the plight of Louisiana's impoverished whites by using divisive and racially charged rhetoric to win their votes. They scapegoated the white citizens' economic stagnation as being the result of both competition with black laborers and corrupt carpetbag rule. They claimed to empathize with poor whites; the whites pledged their votes to the Democrats in response. The Louisiana Constitution of 1879 severely limited the gains of African Americans and moved the state capital from New Orleans to Baton Rouge.

Black reaction to the rise of paramilitary groups such as the White League and the Ku Klux Klan coupled with failures of Reconstruction was powerful. Henry Adams, an ex-slave and Union veteran, organized the Colonization Council in 1874 in an attempt to initiate a mass exodus from Louisiana. He sent agents throughout the state to recruit and inform of his goals. His association was estimated at 92,800 members. The movement, known as "the Exodus" for its biblical implications, attempted unsuccessfully to migrate to Liberia; the would-be emigrants' demands to the federal government went ignored. Leaders of the Exodus shifted their sights instead to a mass migration to Kansas for its vast agricultural opportunities. The movement especially captivated the imaginations of African Americans living in the lower Mississippi River Valley.[196]

In April 1879, as delegates met in New Orleans to finalize the new constitution, another convention was assembling. The Exodus Convention was organized by many influential black activists of the era to coordinate a mass departure from Louisiana's increasingly oppressive political regime. The movement was controversial among people of color and faced resistance from prominent black leaders. One state senator gave a speech outside the convention that almost ignited a riot. P.B.S. Pinchback claimed that proposed migration was misguided and had been organized by illiterate clergy members. Frederick Douglass criticized the movement because it conceded to the notion that "colored people and white people cannot live together in peace and prosperity." A man at the Exodus Convention responded to such criticism by inquiring as to why Douglass himself had left the South yet insisted that others of his own race remain. The inquiry went unanswered. Despite the increasingly hostile racial division in the region, resistance to the migration among whites was surprisingly intense. Planters did not want to see their largest labor force depleted. To incite fear among potential emigrants, planters perpetuated horror stories in local newspapers about northerners threating to shoot "Exodusters" on sight and claimed that the region was being decimated by smallpox. One rumor circulated that Jefferson Davis himself blocked the Mississippi River with ten thousand armed veterans ready to re-enslave migrants.[197]

Migrating anywhere proved challenging for impoverished black Louisianans. To properly relocate required around $700 worth of equipment, supplies and food. Many arrived to their new homes without capital, and federal assistance never materialized. Despite the complications of resettlement, over ten thousand black Louisianans made the arduous journey north during that year. William Ivy Hair noted in *Bourbonism and Agrarian Protest* that the "Exodus of 1879 deserves recognition as one of the most genuine grass-roots upheavals in American history."[198]

THERE WERE SCATTERED episodes of solidarity between black and white Louisianans during this racially tumultuous era. In 1881, in St. Bernard Parish, Gabriel Casanova, an Isleño, is reported to have instigated a substantial labor strike. Backed by other Isleños, he traveled to various plantations and convinced the laborers to cease working in protest for better wages. Reports estimated that at least three hundred black and white laborers joined Casanova's forces to combat poor working conditions. The *Times-Picayune* wrote in an article, "Riot in St. Bernard," about the circumstances:

> *On Monday, however, the strike assumed more serious proportions, verging into a riot. It is stated that about three or four hundred negroes banded together under the leadership of some of the Spaniards, or "Islangs," and went from plantation to plantation, compelling the laborers to stop work until the planters consent to pay the wages demanded....Finding it necessary to quell the turbulent disturbers a committee of planters called at the Governor's office and asked for the authorities of the State to assist them as the parish authorities are powerless.*[199]

The strike garnered national attention, perhaps for the multiracial makeup of its participants. The *Boston Daily Journal* wrote a story claiming "laborers are on a strike in St. Bernard parish" and noted that the "leader of the strike is a white man."[200]

Newspapers reported that since Sheriff Nuñez, an Isleño as well, failed to subdue the strike, Governor Wiltz sent a detachment from the Orleans Artillery to suppress the demonstration. Notably, just thirteen years prior, federal troops had entered St. Bernard Parish to prevent further killings of African Americans by whites, a proportion of whom were Isleños. In 1881, federal troops again were dispatched to St. Bernard Parish, this time to protect the planters' interests as those same ethnic groups marched in solidarity. Serious strikes such as these continued to occur throughout Louisiana, representing a substantial challenge to the status quo in areas where planters had previously maintained supremacy.[201]

LOUISIANA FACED ITS demise from the national spotlight during the Bourbon Era. The year 1880 was New Orleans's final one as one of the nation's top ten most populated cities. During this time, populations rapidly expanded in other cities around the country. Racial violence, although not as severe as the violence that occurred during Reconstruction, also plagued Louisiana during this era.

One episode in particular epitomized the racial tension during the Bourbon Era. In 1893, Victor Estopinal, the man who led armed groups to violence during the St. Bernard Parish Massacre of 1868, was acting as judge in Carrollton, then a separate jurisdiction to New Orleans. The man on trial was Roselius Julian, an African American man accused of beating his wife. Notably, Julian was known to have supported a Republican candidate who lost to Estopinal. During the trial, Julian shot Estopinal twice while Estopinal's back was turned away from Julian. Estopinal charged at his assailant, only to be struck a third time. Estopinal's wife walked in as Julian stood over the injured judge and watched Julian deliver the fourth and fatal shot in the heart.[202]

August Estopinal, a son of Victor Estopinal, chased his father's murderer to his cabin, where Julian reloaded and grabbed a Winchester rifle. Julian shot August twice. August crawled to a nearby house and received medical attention, while Julian escaped to the swamps. His three brothers, mother and sister were arrested a few days later on suspicion of assisting the fugitive.[203]

After news of the attack spread throughout the region, armed groups roamed the swamps in search of Julian, but to no avail. They went to the house of John Willis, Julian's friend, but their interrogation did not yield the

The tombstone of Victor Estopinal and his family in the St. Bernard Cemetery. *Courtesy of Rhett Pritchard.*

desired information. Infuriated, the mob beat Willis to death. After a long day of unsuccessful searching, the crowd convened at the prison to discuss further action. It was there they decided the fate of Julian's imprisoned family, and their decision garnered national attention. The *New York Tribune* provided the following description of the events that unfolded:

About 11 o'clock a body of about twenty-five men, some armed with rifles and shotguns came up to the jail and lit a lantern. They unlocked the door and then held a conference among themselves as to what they should do. Some were in favor of hanging the whole five, while others raised objections and insisted that only two of the brothers, a short one and tall one, Valsin and Bakile, should be taken out and strung up. This was finally agreed to, and several of the men went into the jail, and coming out afterward brought with them the two doomed negroes. They were hurried across to a pasture, 100 yards distant, and there asked to take their last chance of saving their lives by making a confession. The negroes made no reply. They were then told to kneel down and pray. One did so: the other remained standing, but both prayed fervently. The taller negro was then hoisted up. He remained hanging fully five minutes before the second one was hanged. The shorter negro stood gazing at the horrible death of his brother without flinching.[204]

The mob returned to the prison and took Julian's third brother, Paul, and lynched him at Camp Parapet in full view of a crowd as a warning to others. Julian's mother and two sisters were publicly beaten and flogged, after which they were given an hour and a half to leave town. After having witnessed the brutalities inflicted on the Julian family, other African Americans then armed themselves and amassed at Camp Parapet for protection. The episode was one of the most gruesome of the Bourbon Era, excluding the lynching of eleven Italians two years earlier.[205]

As WITH MOST of the American South, violence against African Americans to keep them in their position in St. Bernard Parish came in the form of lynching. There are several recorded accounts of such events. In 1884, two men engaged in a scuffle at the Contreras Plantation, the former plantation of General P.G.T. Beauregard. The conflict ended when Charles Goodman, an African American, shot Louis Maspero, the white owner of the plantation, as Maspero was walking his servant home at night. Charles and his brother, Albert, were lynched as retribution. Albert was not present for the crime but deemed guilty by association. The *Daily Picayune* remarked that the brothers were "launched into eternity from the gallows."[206]

A similar incident occurred in May 1886. Major W.P. Greene, a prominent planter, engaged in an altercation with Robert Smith, a black laborer. The origins of the conflict are unknown, but Smith attacked Greene with a singletree, a bar used in pulling wagons or plows, and caused him to fall. Smith then armed himself with a pistol and went to the house where Greene was eating. As soon as Major Greene opened the door, Smith greeted him with a shot in the abdomen. Smith abandoned the scene, and Greene died at his residence later that night. Smith was eventually captured and imprisoned for the murder of Major Greene. A mob gathered the next morning and battered their way into the prison. Smith was lynched at the nearest tree.[207]

In 1894, another saga in Arabi, an area of St. Bernard Parish closest to New Orleans, captured the attention of the city. George King, a black cattle merchant, was apparently a known fighter in the area with a reputation for getting into scuffles. The *Daily Item* noted that many of the fights were not his fault because they were caused "by the deviltry of St. Bernard residents who knew that the negro was a very ticklish individual and wanted to fight the moment he was poked in the ribs." One such event came to a peak when King threatened a local butcher after a heated exchange. The butcher notified Joseph Guerra, a police officer, and the two men waited for King's reappearance.[208]

King returned to the scene with a shotgun. Guerra drew his gun on King; King fired a shot in response and wounded Guerra in the face. A mob gathered at the scene and started chasing King, who fired at the crowd as he ran to take cover in a nearby barn. The mob proceeded to fire at King each time he presented his face at the barn window. After a half hour, "there was a mob of several hundred people, a large number carrying shotguns and a general demand for the negro's blood was heard." King was eventually wounded in his side, but he did not budge from his position. Throughout the ordeal, King wounded nine members of the mob before the frustrated horde decided to torch the place to "smoke him out." King jumped out of the window as the fire neared him and shot his shotgun into the mob when he landed. King was shot once more, and he fell silent. The crowd cheered.[209]

To the surprise of many, King crawled from his position and ran to the levee. The mob chased him and shot him another time, causing him to fall once again. This time, his substantial injuries prevented his escape. The mob positioned a rope around his neck and dragged him three hundred feet until he was hoisted up the nearest tree. His desperate pleas for mercy were met with scorn and mockery. After his death, his body was cut down, but the heated crowd strung him up once more, this time to a different tree. After he was cut down a second time, the mob "trampled upon" his lifeless corpse. His corpse was then put on display by the "little court house," presumably as a warning to others.[210]

The last recorded lynching in St. Bernard Parish occurred in 1896. Two white women were leaving the Poydras Plantation when they were allegedly attacked by James Dandy, also known as Jim Dazzle by some accounts. Dazzle was caught and imprisoned for the alleged attack. The next morning, a group of about twenty-five men broke into the prison with relative ease, as the jailer was atypically absent from his post. The mob dragged Dazzle from his cell, shot him and strung him up to a nearby tree. Dazzle denied the allegations until his last breath, but the mob was not swayed. He was left swinging until the next morning. According to the *Daily Item*, no arrests were made, "as it would be utterly impossible to fasten the guilt on any particular persons, the firing being so general that it can not be said which shots took effect." It concluded, "Even if any arrests were made no jury could be found to convict anyone, as it is generally considered that the negro deserved his fate." Newspapers concocted clever headlines for its readers to enjoy the story. The *Birmingham State Herald* titled its piece "He'll Dazzle No More. Short Shrift for a Dusky Fiend in St. Bernard Parish, La."[211]

It was during the Bourbon Era that de jure segregation was solidified throughout the South. In 1890, Bourbon Democrats passed the Separate Car Act, which required segregated railway cars. Local resistance to the law in New Orleans orchestrated a plan to challenge the ordinance. The *Comité des Citoyens* (Committee of Citizens), a powerful multiracial group, convinced Homer Plessy, an "octoroon" (someone who is one-eighth African American), to board the "whites only" car in the Ninth Ward of New Orleans, just a few miles from the St. Bernard Parish line. The activists hired a private detective to ensure that Plessy would be charged with violating the Separate Car Act. As expected, he was denied entrance and arrested by the detective. Plessy lost his case against Judge John Howard Ferguson and appealed to the Supreme Court of Louisiana, which denied his appeal. Notably, one of the Louisiana justices who voted to deny the appeal was a member of the Crescent City White League. Plessy and the committee took their appeal to the United States Supreme Court, which agreed to hear the case in 1896.

The Supreme Court ruled seven-to-one in favor of "separate but equal," setting a legal precedent for St. Bernard Parish and the entire South.

Harsh economic conditions of the Bourbon Era impacted both poor African Americans and poor whites, especially in St. Bernard Parish and regions where poverty was already present. One Catholic bishop complained that the new economic conditions amounted to a "new form of slavery for both white and colored people." The improvements that Bourbon Democrats had promised to poor whites failed to materialize. According to Gilbert C. Din in his work *The Canary Islanders of Louisiana*:

> *Distressing economic conditions and rampant racism characterized Louisiana in the late nineteenth century. Depressed agricultural prices and land values continued after Reconstruction. Dishonest methods in sugar and cotton marketing defrauded yeoman farmers of the rewards of their labors. Many small farmers failed and became sharecroppers. Government expenditures declined, and white illiteracy actually rose between 1880 and 1890. Bourbon politicians waved the "bloody shirt" of Reconstruction and exploited the race issue to rally support from lower-class whites.*[212]

The rise of populism addressed these insufferable economic conditions and exposed the divisive tactics of Bourbon Democrats. Lower-class Republicans and Democrats formed alliances, much to the dismay of those in power. Bourbon Democrats faced the startling realization that their voter base was dwindling. In 1892, integrated unions consisting of over three thousand workers went on strike throughout New Orleans to obtain a ten-hour workday with overtime pay. Despite numerous appeals to racial hatred to divide the strikers, the workers stood in solidarity and won almost all of their demands.

Similar episodes became more frequent and increasingly frightened the elite. In the elections of 1896, the Bourbon Democrats desperately resorted to rigging the election, a practice they had decried when employed by Republicans during Reconstruction. If the issue of increasing alliances across racial lines to achieve economic and political rights went unaddressed, the power structure in Louisiana would sway. Bourbons needed to obstruct the voting power of the poor, both black and white. They convened a new constitution to address their crisis and restrict suffrage among poor Louisianans. The constitution of 1898 banned voting for illiterates, issued a poll tax and required grandfather clauses. The black voting bloc declined from 130,000 to a mere 1,342, while the white voting bloc declined from 164,000 to 92,000. By 1910, the number of registered black voters had dropped to 730, less than a half percent of eligible black men. The political voice of the poor was effectively silenced.[213]

Such policies and strife defined the Bourbon age of Louisiana. The poor suffered miserably under economic policies that disproportionately harmed them. Black Americans lost many rights gained during Reconstruction. The influence of Bourbon Democrats lessened at the end of the nineteenth century. As a new century emerged, different entities flexed their muscle. Natural gas and petroleum companies and salt and sulfur companies started to exercise control over the state government. They passed legislation to avoid taxation and regulation while exploiting labor through lower wages and horrid working conditions. This economic activity would both unite Louisiana's working poor and divide them. St. Bernard Parish experienced that rift.

Chapter 8

RECOLLECTION

conomic conditions did improve slightly for some of the Isleños and other impoverished whites during the Bourbon Era; however, it was hardly due to the Bourbon policies. During this era, facets of the Industrial Revolution reached lower St. Bernard Parish as newer innovations were introduced. More railroads were built, roads were improved and some people embraced the concept of obtaining a formal education to improve their economic position. However, others continued to work as their ancestors did and regarded education as an impractical solution out of poverty or unnecessary as they were complacent with their way of life.[214]

Despite improvements, visitors remarked about the archaic lifestyle of the Isleños. In 1891, Alcée Fortier, a Louisiana historian, took the newly built New Orleans and Shell Beach Railroad. He discussed his two-hour journey:

> Our train passed through historic ground, for shortly after leaving the city we saw the plain of Chalmette, where Wellington's veterans were defeated by Jackson and his brave troops, among whom were many Louisiana Creoles. We saw the charred ruins of Villere's house where were established Pakenham's headquarters; we looked with sorrow and shame at the monument erected to Jackson on the battle field, and which stands dilapidated and unfinished. We crossed the canals and bayous by which the British troops had come from the lakes; we passed Poydras plantation, which had belonged to the poet, statesman and philanthropist, the friend of the sick, of the orphans and of indigent girls.[215]

Chalmette Monument after its completion, circa 1910. *Courtesy of the Library of Congress.*

Fortier continued on the economic condition of the Isleños:

> *A number of these people are men of education and of some wealth; the senator from St. Bernard parish is an Estopinal and the sheriff is a Nuñez. The great majority, however, as with descendants of the Acadians, are poor and ignorant. They cultivate their little patch of ground and raise vegetables, chiefly potatoes and onions. They are also great hunters. They all speak Spanish, but a few speak the Creole patois and the younger ones speak English. The language is not as corrupt as might be expected.*[216]

Fortier spoke with an illiterate elderly woman in Spanish. She was fluent in Spanish and French. She bemoaned the youth's preference to attempt English over their native tongue. When Fortier apologized for bothering her with questions, she responded, "*Nada, seño (señor); al contrario, me alegro mucho de su visita; me ha alegrado el corason (corazon).*" Fortier's translation: "Not at all, sir; on the contrary, your visit pleases me very much; it has pleased my heart."[217]

Fortier made a second visit the same year and stayed on Ben Olivier's plantation, which he described as "one of the oldest and most distinguished in Louisiana." After detailing their royal ancestry, he visited Delacroix Island, which he referred to as "*l'Ile*." He wrote:

> *The dwellings are on both sides of the bayous and are mostly palmetto huts. As it was a cold day nearly all the men had gone hunting and fishing, and the women were indoors; a few children, however, dark-haired and brown, were running about in the cold wind, bareheaded and barefooted, and a young man in a canoe was crossing the bayou in the direction of a hut....*
>
> *The Spaniards on* l'Ile *live entirely by hunting and fishing. The women fish in the bayou in front of their huts, but the men go to the gulf for fishing and to the lakes for hunting. They bring back immense quantities of fish and ducks, which are sent to the Olivier railroad station, ten or twelve miles distant, in small carts drawn by oxen, yoked Spanish fashion, by the horns....The palmetto huts struck me with amazement—how could human beings in a civilized country live in such dwellings!*[218]

Fortier often compared the rural life to an industrious and more modern New Orleans with pretention. In Delacroix, he met with Mr. Pepe, a patriarch of the island, to discuss the customs of the island. Mr. Pepe claimed no one in the region was literate. (This illiteracy probably contributed to the lack of written records from the perpetrators and victims of the St. Bernard Parish Massacre.) Fortier wrote, "They lived without the schoolmaster and physician, and only needed the priest for marriage and funeral ceremonies." He referenced their racial beliefs: "The Isleños are a pure race; they have a perfect horror of the negro and marry among themselves." He noted that the "women are rather handsome and are very dark." Mr. Pepe sung Fortier a *décima*, a popular poetic song among the Isleños featuring complex rhymes in ten-line stanzas. Mr. Pepe stated that he did not desire more in life than beans, coffee and bread.[219]

People of lower St. Bernard Parish also had to contend with the harsh elements of nature. In 1892, the Mississippi River flooded and resulted in loss of property in Terre-aux-Bouefs. Hurricanes in 1893, 1901 and 1909 continually devastated fragile structures on the water. The hurricane of 1893, known as the Great October Storm, bombarded lower St. Bernard Parish as it made its way to the island of Chenière Caminada. The storm completely decimated the island and resulted in over two thousand total deaths, making it one of the country's deadliest hurricanes.[220]

Education improved throughout the parish. Although schools existed in upper St. Bernard Parish, Delacroix Island opened its first schoolhouse in 1894. In 1902, its teachers were paid $12.50 a month. Despite educational progress, school enrollment was slow. In 1906, only 328 white and 46 black students were enrolled in school. In 1907, the parish had six white and two black schools. An eighth-grade education was the highest achievement. Outstanding students went elsewhere to continue their studies. A few males even received scholarships to Louisiana State University or Tulane University. Excelling females were sent to two-year teacher training programs.[221]

ECONOMIC PROGRESS OCCURRED throughout the parish as outsiders sought to exploit the parish's vast resources. In 1886, the construction of the Violet Canal connected the Mississippi River to Lake Borgne. It was expanded in 1900. The community of Violet developed around the canal. Italians continued to immigrate to the parish to sell their labor, just as they did during Reconstruction. Our Lady of Lourdes Church was built in 1916 to serve the growing population, and sermons varied between three languages: Italian, French and English. Newspapers referred to the area as having an "Italian colony." In 1907, the Chalmette Slip opened to provide the parish with a deep-draft harbor, followed by new massive tanks constructed by Standard Oil.[222]

Arabi experienced the largest increase in economic activity, perhaps due to its proximity to New Orleans and its already bustling local economy complete with slaughterhouses, cattle pens and dockyards. In the 1880s, Arabi became part of St. Bernard Parish to avoid the regulations on slaughterhouses. The town named itself after Ahmed 'Urabi, an Egyptian who fought for independence against Great Britain in the early 1880s. Local newspapers often misspelled 'Urabi as Arabi. The political and business leaders of Arabi likened themselves to his struggle as they fought to become independent from New Orleans's increasing regulations. Prior to this renaming, the area was referred to as Stocklanding. In 1909, the American Sugar Refining Company completed the largest sugar refinery in the world in Arabi. The same year, the *St. Bernard Voice* also announced the construction of a cypress mill. In 1914, the building of an automobile plant was announced. Collectively, these industries would employ thousands.[223]

Archaic industries suffered as the newer ones dominated the region. By the early twentieth century, the catfish industry reported abysmal gains in comparison to earlier years despite the plentiful amount of catfish caught by

"The Crescent City Live Stock Landing and Slaughter House Company" in contemporary Old Arabi, 1874. *Courtesy of the New Orleans Historic Collection.*

fishermen. The fishermen claimed it was due to the newer occupations as the workers "employed at the industries now in operation in St. Bernard do not leave the premises until knocking-off time, when they go straight home." In 1910, the parish's last sugar mill was removed. Locally grown sugar would be exported elsewhere on newer railroads and paved roads. Many plantations that once epitomized the glamour and wealth of renowned families and elites were destroyed or remained idle and decrepit.[224]

The progress St. Bernard Parish experienced in the early twentieth century was halted by a catastrophic hurricane in 1915. Property throughout the parish was destroyed, and it was felt hardest among the poor in lower St. Bernard Parish. Many Isleños and African Americans lost everything. The Filipino settlement of Saint Malo was permanently obliterated, as were remnants of Bas du Fleuve and other colonies along Lake Borgne. New businesses in Arabi closed due to heavy losses, and unemployment surged. Newly built schools were in ruins. At least thirty people died, although that is likely an underestimated figure.[225]

WORLD WAR I also upended normalcy as it flung many of the "local boys beyond the marsh" into Europe. According to Samantha Perez in *The Isleños of Louisiana*, "Various disasters, both natural and political, forcefully tossed many Isleños headfirst into modernity." Over five hundred St. Bernard Parish men of various races registered for the draft. The parish united and rallied behind them. Some, such as Isleño Joachim Sanchez Jr., did not return. On August 17, 1919, the parish held a welcome home ceremony in Arabi for the returning participants. The Great War brought some of the parish's most impoverished to vast regions of the world more than ever before in the parish's long history. After the war, the "pace of life" accelerated in the region.[226]

Ten days after that celebration and in the same hall, striking butchers met with the New Orleans Live Stock Exchange in an attempt to reach an agreement. The unionized butchers did not agree to temporarily work during the strike to slaughter the remaining cows. The New Orleans Live Stock Exchange threatened to bring in nonunion labor to slaughter the cows before they "deteriorate." The machinists' and engineers' union stood in solidarity with the butchers' union and threatened to cut the supply of light and water if nonunion labor was employed. The unions eventually won their demands.[227]

Less than a year later, forty black and white butchers at the St. Bernard Rendering and Fertilizing Company went on strike to increase their pay by a dollar a day. The company refused to recognize the union because it claimed it wanted to treat its workers as "individuals." The company employed nonunion workers as the strike ensued. Newspapers claimed the strike almost led to riots between union workers and their temporary replacements. The secretary-treasurer had a bullet graze his head during an ambush by the strikers. Several black workers were arrested in retaliation. After four months, the strikers won some of the demands and saw their pay increase along with collective bargaining rights.[228]

Biracial strikes for better worker conditions were common throughout the era, but their successes faded at the onset of the 1920s due to the economic prosperity of industrial powerhouses and the subsequent weakening of unions. One of the largest biracial strikes in the parish's history occurred at the American Sugar Refinery in 1920. Over four hundred white and black workers went on strike for union recognition and better wages; they resorted to violence at times. In February 1920, strikers boarded and attacked workers on streetcars traveling to the refinery with the justification that the workers were strikebreakers. Violence escalated in one of the streetcars, and an African American worker was shot in the head and killed by a striker. The streetcars halted, and workers returned home instead of work, causing the refinery to temporarily close down. A month later, the *New Orleans States* reported that streetcars refused to enter Arabi out of fear of strikers. Strikers also roamed around the refinery and scuffled with police and watchmen. The strike, despite employing all efforts, did not succeed, as the strikers were eventually replaced with relative ease with desperate laborers.[229]

As St. Bernard Parish progressed into modernity, the chaotic events of 1868 faded from collective memory. Other events replaced the memories of the residents. During Prohibition, the waterways of lower St. Bernard Parish became a corridor for the illegal importation of alcohol; humble men became wealthy by importing the desired poisons to a thirsty New Orleans. In 1922, the Mississippi River flooded lower St. Bernard Parish, and approximately two thousand inhabitants immediately lost their homes. In 1926, Isleño trappers engaged in a battle, known as the Trappers' War, with men who tried to control the territory the Isleños had occupied for well over a century. Less than a year later, the government blew up the levees during the Great Mississippi River Flood of 1927 to save New Orleans, flooding lower St. Bernard Parish and leaving thousands homeless once again. The victims were never adequately compensated.

As St. Bernard Parish continued throughout the century, it was faced with ceaseless calamities that changed its character. The Great Depression hit St. Bernard Parish, as with most areas of Louisiana, hard. Fur was not in vogue, which caused the profits of trappers to decrease. Hurricanes and flooding continually ravaged lower St. Bernard Parish. White flight from New Orleans in 1960s altered the demographics and solidified a white majority. The relentless flooding from Hurricane Katrina that obliterated almost everything in its path rudely welcomed St. Bernard Parish to the twenty-first century. Overall, the St. Bernard Parish Massacre and its impact

An African American man working outside the old slave quarters, circa 1930s. Many African Americans lived on the property of plantations for decades after the abolishment of slavery. *Courtesy of the State Library of Louisiana.*

on the parish's character became more distant as the voices of the era began to disappear and newer events took precedent.

Today, most St. Bernard Parish residents are unaware of the massacre. Many of the participants on both sides were illiterate and relied on others to transcribe their stories. Those capable of providing oral history accounts were rarely consulted, much less interviewed. Local documents were repeatedly lost due to negligence or from hurricanes and floods, with the last documents lost during Hurricane Katrina. The massacre is almost entirely lost through oral tradition. It was discussed in black churches until the 1990s. One pastor and community leader, the late Reverend Samuel Smith II, evoked the massacre in his sermons at First Baptist Church in Verret, located in the vicinity of the mayhem. The church was founded by Smith's grandfather in 1871, and Smith's son Reverend Raymond Smith is the current pastor. Reverend Samuel Smith II's oral account of the massacre was recorded before his death, but it washed away during Hurricane Katrina. His account was arguably one of the last traces of any oral history of the event from St. Bernard Parish's black community.

I sat down with Jerry Estopinal at the Los Isleños Heritage and Multi-Cultural Museum in lower St. Bernard Parish. Jerry is a direct descendant of Victor and Francis Estopinal, two of the men who participated in the massacre. His grandfather's godfather was Albert Estopinal, the Confederate veteran and politician. I asked Jerry about aspects of oral history that he could recall from his family. He was familiar with the story of Pablo San Feliu but had heard various accounts of the story. "I heard as a child that they had killed Pablo San Feliu, and that up and down what is today Bayou Road down here…that they had riders up and down." He knew from "what the old people would tell" that there was violence at that time, but he was unsure about any details.[230]

I asked him how the community could better remember the massacre. According to Jerry, "There needs to be some type of memorial.…They do need something. And it needs to be just a much better understanding of how all these groups get involved, and then you got these different people in government that are trying to manipulate all these people. Probably does sound familiar." He summed up his views about the event in one word: "tragedy."[231]

I wanted to speak to a descendant of one of the victims; however, connecting people today to those killed proved an impossible task. Although there are similarities in a few surnames, I could not ascertain direct connections due to lost or destroyed ancestral records. To my knowledge, all of the freedpeople killed were formerly enslaved, and the only ones mentioned were the few in Lieutenant J.M. Lee's report.

Similar to many antebellum records in St. Bernard Parish, many of the aforementioned physical places are lost to history. In 1964, the National Park Service began demolition of the community of Fazendeville to expand the Chalmette Battlefield. The community had survived the violence of Reconstruction, the dreads of the Great Depression, African American migrations, the catastrophic devastation from hurricanes and the division of the Jim Crow era. The residents were not adequately compensated, and many moved to New Orleans's Lower Ninth Ward. The residents reopened their church, Battle Ground Baptist Church, on Flood Street. Although much of the Lower Ninth Ward was devastated by Hurricane Katrina, it is still in operation as of writing this work. The freedpeople cemetery located near Fazendeville, which was established in 1867 by the Freedmen's Bureau, gradually faded to the elements.

Battle Ground Baptist Church was built in New Orleans's Lower Ninth Ward after its demolition from Fazendeville. *Author's collection.*

Fazendeville prior to its demolition, circa 1960. *Credit to the Louisiana National Guard.*

I sat down with Peter Pierre in Meraux, a suburb in St. Bernard Parish, to discuss that event and the legacy of African American history in St. Bernard Parish. Pierre, born in 1942, resided in Fazendeville until its demolition. Pierre's grandfather Eugene Pierre was born during slavery in 1863. We sifted through his ancestral records, peered over census data and discussed his upbringing in Fazendeville and experiences growing up in St. Bernard Parish. I first asked him about life in Fazendeville. He spoke fondly of a loving community where everyone knew one another and reminisced about playing with friends, "catching crawfish in ponds," hunting rabbits in the nearby woods and taking "fruit from Mrs. Bonnie's" trees.[232]

Pierre's mannerisms changed as he discussed experiences outside Fazendeville. According to Pierre, African Americans were treated as "second-class citizens" and often faced discrimination. He spoke of bars and restaurants where he would have to enter through the back. Pierre remarked:

> *Everything was segregated down here....Blacks, we couldn't go into nothing down here. Everything you had to go to you had to go to New Orleans, but you could work for people down here....I was really something....Different times, different people. You would hear the "n" word. In that little town of Fazendeville, the police hardly ever come in there though.*[233]

That harsh mentality is what led to the demolition of the black community. The decision to demolish the community came at the start of school integration and white flight. According to Pierre:

I was old enough to know why. I just think that they wanted black people out. Take ya, shift ya and force ya out....I knew it was a racial thing behind it, ya know? Just get black people away from there, ya know? You see, at the time, they built that subdivision across the back part of Fazendeville, Buccaneer Villa. They just built that, and I thought that was another reason why they figured blacks that lived over there were too close to that subdivision.[234]

I then discussed with him in length the events of 1868. He knew of racial violence during that time but was unfamiliar with any details. I asked, "How do you think our parish or our community can memorialize the victims who fell in 1868?" Pierre said it should be incorporated into United States history. He elaborated, "I think they should build some kind of memorial. Something. And I don't know if they could pay their descendants any sort of restitution depending on how it went down."[235]

The majority of people I have talked with about this event reiterated similar sentiment: they want to see it memorialized or recognized in some manner. There is no marker or plaque, as with other historically significant events. Many of the physical reminders of the tragedy are lost to history. Florey's Coffeehouse, the makeshift prison used during the massacre, burned down sometime in the 1970s. Toca, the area around Philippe Toca's residence, is named after him and heavily used in the lexicon of parish residents today. Philippe Toca, similar to other participants, is buried in the St. Bernard Cemetery across from the St. Bernard Catholic Church. Much that survived to the twenty-first century was destroyed by Hurricane Katrina. The only physical reminder of the event is the tombstone of Pablo San Feliu, located a few tombstones from Toca's. It reads:

Pablo San Feliu
Assassinated by Slaves
Incited by Carpetbag Rule
Died Oct. 1869

The mismarked epithet has many implications. Dates were not kept well among the poor in St. Bernard Parish, and the "1869" date gives credence to the notion that it was erected a significant time after, as the story passed through oral tradition. The usage of "assassination" implies San Feliu was of some importance to the community. It also implies he was not at fault. Those who erected the tomb still considered freedpeople "slaves" or they could not recall if slavery was formally abolished yet. They also appropriated blame on carpetbaggers, the aforementioned derogatory term given to people from the North who migrated south during Reconstruction, for inciting the violence.

According to William Hyland, the current St. Bernard Parish historian, the tombstone was probably erected under the auspices of Leander Perez, a wealthy businessman and ardent segregationist who ruled St. Bernard Parish and Plaquemines Parish as his fiefdoms during the mid-twentieth century.

Victor Estopinal, despite being murdered outside St. Bernard Parish, is buried with much of his family a few tombstones away from Feliu. Other participants are buried in the same cemetery. The freedpeople were most likely buried in a cemetery that did not survive the test of time.

Some notable events discussed in earlier chapters do have markers. There is a plaque dedicated to the Colfax Massacre. There is a statue commemorating the Battle of Liberty Place that was relegated from the center of Canal Street to a less-traveled corridor in the French Quarter. It was added during the Bourbon Era to honor those who temporarily overthrew the Reconstruction government. In 2015, the New Orleans City Council declared it a nuisance and set up for its removal. The decision included the removal of three other statues: the General P.G.T. Beauregard Equestrian

The tombstone of Philippe Toca. *Courtesy of Rhett Pritchard.*

The headstone of Pablo San Feliu in St. Bernard Cemetery. *Courtesy of Rhett Pritchard.*

The grave of Pablo San Feliu in St. Bernard Cemetery. *Author's collection.*

A memorial in St. Bernard Cemetery dedicated to St. Bernardians who fought in both World War I and World War II. *Courtesy of Rhett Pritchard.*

Statues of angels mark the entrance to St. Bernard Cemetery. *Courtesy of Rhett Pritchard.*

Statue, the Robert E. Lee Monument and the Jefferson Davis Monument. In 2017, the city commenced their removal, starting with the Battle of Liberty Place memorial first.

I ASKED SAMANTHA Perez, author of *The Isleños of Louisiana: On the Water's Edge*, how we can better memorialize this event in our regional history and how we can remember the victims as we remember the victims of other tragedies. Dr. Perez is a local historian who grew up in St. Bernard Parish and has taken a keen interest in the region's history. Her book is one of the only works that gives the massacre noteworthy attention. Dr. Perez eloquently responded:

> *The best way to honor history is to learn from it. We should not shy away from our history, even the parts that make us uncomfortable, in conversations, in public discourse or in the classroom—especially in the classroom. The next generation should always be aware of the specific problems their community has faced and overcome so they can be better prepared to confront contemporary concerns and positively overcome those too.*
>
> *A plaque or a memorial are wonderful ways to honor the past and inform viewers of what has value to the people who erected it, but I think what recent debates concerning the removal of Civil War–era statues has suggested is that a statue is still an object, whatever extra cultural meaning we attribute to it, that only really affects those who see the thing. It's the memory of the event that matters, and what we do with that memory—how we learn from the past, all of the past—that matters most.*[236]

As a history teacher in St. Bernard Parish, I try to incorporate the St. Bernard Parish Massacre, along with similar events, in the curriculum and in lessons so that students are aware of their history and its relevance to their lives. This massacre solidified white supremacy in the parish at a time when a marginalized group finally gained long-withheld freedoms and suffrage (for males). It helped determine policies and impacted the trajectory of the region for well over a century. It is important to never forget those who paid the ultimate sacrifice at the hands of greedy and misguided individuals. Furthermore, it's imperative that history teaches us the devastating results of appropriating blame for economic concerns on those who are different and to be suspicious of those who seek to divide for their own advancement.

Perhaps Ceceil George, the enslaved woman who was sold to a planter in St. Bernard Parish, best captures the essence of hope in dire times. While she was enslaved in the "ole country," they sang a song called "Inching Along" to pass the time as they worked. She sang it to conclude her interview; I will use an excerpt to conclude this work:

I'm inchin' along, inchin' along
Jesus is comin', bye an' bye!
Like de pore lowly worm,
I'm inchin' along,
Jesus is comin' bye an' bye!

When I was a sinner, jus' like yo'.
Jesus is comin', bye an' bye!
I did not know, what I could do 'cause
Jesus is comin' bye an' bye.

With worry I was like some one dead,
Jesus is comin' bye an' bye;
An ache in my heart, an ache in my head.
Jesus is comin' bye an' bye

I prayed over her', an' I pray over there
Jesus is comin' bye an' bye!
I prayed over yonder, then I stopped to ponder
Jesus is comin' bye an' bye!

I went on da wall to repent an' pray
Jesus is comin' bye an' bye!
An' I know my sin must be washed away,
Jesus is comin' bye an' bye.[237]

NOTES

Introduction

1. First Lieutenant J.M. Lee, Thirty-Ninth U.S. Infantry, *St. Bernard Riot, 1868* (New Orleans, LA, November 27, 1868), 28.
2. Ibid.
3. Louisiana Congress, *Supplemental Report of Joint Committee of the General Assembly of Louisiana, On the Conduct of the Late Elections and the Condition of Peace and Good Order in the State* (New Orleans: A.L. Lee, State Printer, 1869), vi–vii, books.google.com/books?id=j9A-AAAAYAAJ&printsec=frontcover#v=onepage&q=riot&f=false.

Chapter 1

4. George Washington Cable, *Creoles and Cajuns: Stories of Old Louisiana*, ed. Arlin Turner (New York: Doubleday Anchor Books, 1959), 418–19.
5. Gilbert C. Din, *Spaniards, Planters, and Slaves: The Spanish Regulation of Slavery in Louisiana, 1763–1803* (College Station: Texas A&M University Press, 1999), 104–5.
6. Lawrence N. Powell, *The Accidental City: Improvising New Orleans* (Cambridge, MA: Harvard University Press, 2013), 238; Din, *Spaniards, Planters, and Slaves*, 95.

7. Samuel Wilson Jr., *The Battle of New Orleans: Plantation Houses on the Battlefield of New Orleans* (n.p.: Louisiana Landmarks Society), 6; Ned Sublette, *The World that Made New Orleans: From Spanish Silver to Congo Square* (Chicago: Chicago Review Press, n.d.), 59.

8. Gwendolyn Midlo Hall, *Africans in Colonial Louisiana: The Development of Afro-Creole Culture in the Eighteenth Century* (Baton Rouge: Louisiana State University Press, 1995), 203.

9. Sublette, *World that Made New Orleans*, 112; Daniel Rasmussen, *American Uprising: The Untold Story of America's Largest Slave Revolt* (New York: Harper Perennial, 2012), 88; Din, *Spaniards, Planters, and Slaves*, 98; Hall, *Africans in Colonial Louisiana*, 213.

10. Powell, *Accidental City*, 244.

11. Ibid., 245; Din, *Spaniards, Planters, and Slaves*, 103.

12. Powell, *Accidental City*, 248.

13. Lafcadio Hearn, "Saint Malo," *Harper's Weekly*, vol. 27, March 31, 1883.

14. Samantha Perez, *The Isleños of Louisiana: On the Water's Edge* (Charleston, SC: The History Press, 2011), 12.

15. Hall, *Africans in Colonial Louisiana*, 207.

16. Gilbert C. Din, *The Canary Islanders of Louisiana* (Baton Rouge: Louisiana State University Press, 1999), 15–16.

17. Perez, *Isleños of Louisiana*, 12, 52.

18. Ibid., 34.

19. Din, *Canary Islanders of Louisiana*, 51.

20. Ibid., 48–52.

21. Ibid., 52–53.

22. Ibid., 54.

23. Ibid., 55; Perez, *Isleños of Louisiana*, 35.

24. George Morrison Rolph, *Something about Sugar: Its History, Growth, Manufacture and Distribution* (n.p.: J.J. Newbegin, 1917), 176–77; Marie Louise Points, "St. Bernard Parish: A Suburb of New Orleans Full of Historical Interest," *Daily Picayune*, January 13, 1895, 23.

25. Din, *Canary Islanders of Louisiana*, 117.

26. Ibid., 59–60.

27. Ibid., 60.

28. Robert V. Remini, *The Battle of New Orleans: Andrew Jackson and America's First Military Victory* (New York: Penguin Books, 2001), 24.

29. Ibid., 28, 33.

30. Ibid., 34–36, 47–49.

31. Ibid., 58.

32. Ibid., 38.

33. Ibid., 54, 62; Arsène Lacarrière, *Historical Memoir of the War in West Florida and Louisiana in 1814–15*, expanded edition (New Orleans: Historic New Orleans Collection, 1999), 82–83.

34. Remini, *Battle of New Orleans*, 66–70.

35. Ibid., 68–69.

36. Din, *Canary Islanders of Louisiana*, 92.

37. James Parton, *Life of Andrew Jackson* (Boston: Houghton, Mifflin and Company, 1888), 126–27.

38. Louise McKinney, *New Orleans: A Cultural History* (Oxford, UK: Oxford University Press, 2006), 17.

39. Remini, *Battle of New Orleans*, 70.

40. Vincent Nolte, *Fifty Years in Both Hemispheres: Reminiscences of the Life of a Former Merchant* (New York: Redfield, 1854), 177.

41. Ron Chapman, *The Battle of New Orleans: But for a Piece of Wood* (Gretna, LA: Pelican Publishing Company, 2013), 138.

42. George Washington Cable, *Creole Slave Songs* (New York: Century Co., 1886), 815.

Chapter 2

43. Wilson, *Battle of New Orleans*, 27; Harriet Martineau, *Retrospect of Western Travel*, vol. 2 (London: Saunders and Otley, Conduit-Street, 1838), 155.

44. Walter Pritchard, ed., "Some Interesting Glimpses of Louisiana a Century Ago," *Louisiana Historical Quarterly* (1941): 43–48.

45. Din, *Canary Islanders of Louisiana*, 93.

46. Ibid., 102.

47. Ibid., 100–3.

48. Ceceil George, in Ronnie W. Clayton, ed., *Mother Wit: The Ex-Slave Narratives of the Louisiana Writers' Project* (New York, 1990), 83.

49. Ibid., 84.

50. John C. Rodrigue, *Reconstruction in the Cane Fields: From Slavery to Free Labor in Louisiana's Sugar Parishes, 1862–1880* (Baton Rouge: Louisiana State University Press, 2001), 21–22; 2004 Historical Census Browser, retrieved September 24, 2015, from the University of Virginia, Geospatial and Statistical Data Center, mapserver.lib.virginia.edu/collections.

51. Rodrigue, *Reconstruction in the Cane Fields*, 11.

52. Charles P. Roland, *Louisiana Sugar Plantations During the Civil War* (Baton Rouge: Louisiana State University Press, 1997), 22–23.

53. Din, *Canary Islanders of Louisiana*, 105–6.

54. Ella Lonn, *Foreigners in the Confederacy*, 1st ed. (Chapel Hill: University of North Carolina Press, 2002), 147; Jacek Praga and Wiesław Wróblewski, *United Poles in America* (Ames: Iowa State University, 2002), 33.

55. Din, *Canary Islanders of Louisiana*, 105, 113.

56. T. Harry Williams, *P.G.T. Beauregard: Napoleon in Gray* (Baton Rouge: Louisiana State University Press, 1955), 2–5.

57. *Daily Picayune*, "Meeting in St. Bernard," June 27, 1848, 2.

58. John D. Winters and T. Harry Williams, *The Civil War in Louisiana* (Baton Rouge: Louisiana State University Press, 1991), 25.

59. Ibid., 25–26.

60. Din, *Canary Islanders of Louisiana*, 110.

61. Ibid., 110.

62. Winters and Williams, *Civil War in Louisiana*, 56, 82.

63. Ibid., 82; Dale A. Somers, *The Rise of Sports in New Orleans: 1850–1900* (New Orleans: Pelican Publishing Company, 1971), 76.

64. Michael D. Pierson, *Mutiny at Fort Jackson: The Untold Story of the Fall of New Orleans* (Chapel Hill: University of North Carolina, 2008), 58–60.

65. Ibid., 60–61.

66. Harnett Kane, *Deep Delta Country* (New York: Duell, Sloan & Pearce, 1994), 64.

67. Albert Patterson, in Ronnie W. Clayton, ed., *Mother Wit: The Ex-Slave Narratives of the Louisiana Writers' Project* (New York, 1990), 179.

68. Winters and Williams, *Civil War in Louisiana*, 95–96.

69. Terry L. Jones, "The Fall of New Orleans," *New York Times*, April 25, 2012.

70. Lawrence Van Alstyne, *Diary of an Enlisted Man* (New York: Tuttle, Morehouse & Taylor Company, 1910), 81.

71. Ibid., 82.

72. Ibid., 85.

73. John M. Sacher, "Civil War in Louisiana," KnowLA Encyclopedia of Louisiana, January 6, 2011, accessed February 5, 2015, www.knowla.org/entry/536; Richard Nelson Current, *Lincoln's Loyalists: Union Soldiers from the Confederacy* (n.p.: Northeastern, 1992), 218.

74. George, *Mother Wit*, 85.

75. Moon-Ho Jung, *Coolies and Cane: Race, Labor, and Sugar in the Age of Emancipation* (Baltimore, MD: Johns Hopkins University Press, 2008), 52.

76. Rodrigue, *Reconstruction in the Cane Fields*, 34.

77. Ibid., 22, 34.

78. Ibid., 35.

79. Emancipation Proclamation, January 1, 1863, Presidential Proclamations, 1791–1991, Record Group 11, General Records of the United States Government, National Archives.

80. Din, *Canary Islanders of Louisiana*, 118.

81. Ibid., 106.

82. Williams, *P.G.T. Beauregard*, 262–65.

83. *Daily Picayune*, September 28, 1865, 2.

84. Din, *Canary Islanders of Louisiana*, 112, 116.

85. Virginia Mescher, "How Sweet It Is: A Story of Sugar and Sugar Refining in the United States, Including a Glossary of Sweeteners," January 10, 2005.

86. U.S. Congress, *Testimony Taken by the Committee of Elections, Louisiana*, 1870, 41st Congress, 107, books.google.com/books?id=oO5XAAAAcAAJ&printsec=frontcover&source=gbs_ge_summary_r&cad=0#v=onepage&q&f=false.

Chapter 3

87. Richard Campanella, "Fazendeville and Three Oaks: Reflecting on Two Cultural Losses 150 Years after Battle of New Orleans Victory," Preservation Resource Center of New Orleans, March 2015, 13.

88. Ibid., 13–14.

89. Ronald H. Bayor, *The Columbia Documentary History of Race and Ethnicity in America* (New York: Columbia University Press, 2004), 295.

90. Records of the Assistant Commissioner for the State of Louisiana, Bureau of Refugees, Freedmen and Abandoned Lands, 1865–1869, National Archives Microfilm M1027 Roll 34, Records Relating to Murders and Outrages, "Miscellaneous Reports and Lists Relating to Murders and Outrages, Mar. 1867–Nov. 1868," December 25, 1866, accessed September 14, 2015, freedmensbureau.com/louisiana/outrages/outrages4.htm.

91. Caryn Cossé Bell, *Revolution, Romanticism, and the Afro-Creole Protest Tradition in Louisiana, 1718–1868* (Baton Rouge: Louisiana State University Press, 1997), 262.

92. *New Orleans Tribune*, "Meeting at the Parish of St. Bernard," May 15, 1867, 4.

93. Leopold Guichard, "Freedom Vs. Outrages," *New Orleans Tribune*, June 15, 1867, 4.

94. Rodrigue, *Reconstruction in the Cane Fields*, 86; U.S. Congress, *Testimony Taken by the Committee of Elections, Louisiana*, 107.

95. Rodrigue, *Reconstruction in the Cane Fields*, 99.

96. James Alex Baggett, *The Scalawags: Southern Dissenters in the Civil War and Reconstruction* (Baton Rouge: Louisiana State University Press, 2004), 142.

97. *Daily Picayune*, "Riot in St. Bernard Parish: Democratic Barbecue Broken Up by Radicals—One Person Shot and a Number Severely Beaten," April 14, 1868, 1.

98. Lee, *St. Bernard Riot*, 3.

99. Ibid., 3; U.S. Congress, *Testimony Taken by the Committee of Elections, Louisiana*, 103.

100. U.S. Congress, *Testimony Taken by the Committee of Elections, Louisiana*, 112.

101. U.S. Congress, *Louisiana Contested Elections*, January 1, 1870, 41st Congress, 2nd sess., 1869–70, 630, books.google.com/books?id=oO5XAAAAcAAJ&pg=PA630&lpg=PA630#v=onepage&q&f=false.

102. U.S. Congress, *Testimony Taken by the Committee of Elections, Louisiana*, 104; Lee, *St. Bernard Riot*, 3–4.

103. Ted Tunnell, *Crucible of Reconstruction: War, Radicalism, and Race in Louisiana, 1862–1877* (Baton Rouge: Louisiana State University Press, 1992), 153; Lee, *St. Bernard Riot*, 5; U.S. Congress, *Testimony Taken by the Committee of Elections, Louisiana*, 103.

104. Lee, *St. Bernard Riot*, 5–6.

105. Ibid., 6.

Chapter 4

106. Ibid., 6, 26.

107. Ibid., 25.

108. Ibid., 7.

109. Ibid., 42.

110. U.S. Congress, *Louisiana Contested Elections*, 253.

111. Lee, *St. Bernard Riot*, 7–8.

112. Ibid.

113. Ibid., 8, 30.

114. Testimony of Thomas Ong, *Supplemental Report of Joint Committee of the General Assembly of Louisiana on the Conduct of the Late Elections*.

115. Lee, *St. Bernard Riot*, 9.

116. Ibid., 10.

117. Testimony of John B. Jacques, *Supplemental Report of Joint Committee of the General Assembly of Louisiana on the Conduct of the Late Elections*, 230; Lee, *St. Bernard Riot*, 10–22.

118. Ibid., 11.

119. Ibid.; U.S. Congress, *Testimony Taken by the Committee of Elections, Louisiana*, 104.

120. Testimony of H.M. Whittemore, *Supplemental Report of Joint Committee of the General Assembly of Louisiana on the Conduct of the Late Elections*, 232–33; U.S. Congress, *Testimony Taken by the Committee of Elections, Louisiana*, 106.

121. Lee, *St. Bernard Riot*, 11.

122. Ibid., 11–12.

123. Ibid., 13–15; U.S. Congress, *Testimony Taken by the Committee of Elections, Louisiana*, 105.

124. Lee, *St. Bernard Riot*, 15.

125. Ibid., 15–16.

126. Ibid., 27–28.

127. *Columbus Daily Enquirer*, "Night Dispatches," October 27, 1868, 3.

128. *New York Herald*, "The State of Affairs in Louisiana," October 27, 1868, 6.

129. Ibid.; *New Orleans Bee*, "Negro Riot in St. Bernard Parish," Tuesday morning, October 27, 1868.

130. *Louisiana Democrat*, November 2, 1868, image 2, chroniclingamerica. loc.gov/lccn/sn82003389/1868-11-02/ed-1/seq-2/#date1=1868&index=2&rows=20&words=Bernard+parish+Parish+St&searchType=basic &sequence=0&state=&date2=1868&proxtext=st.+bernard+parish&y= 0&x=0&dateFilterType=yearRange&page=1.

131. Ibid.

132. Ibid.

133. U.S. Congress, *Message of the President of the United States and Accompanying Documents*, 1868, 40th Congress, 3rd Session, 1868, vol. 1, 306, books. google.com/books?id=Gp0dAQAAIAAJ&pg=PA306&lpg=PA306&dq.

134. *New Orleans Republican*, October 26, 1868, Evening, Image 1.

135. Ibid.

136. William Hyland (St. Bernard Parish historian), interviewed by C. Dier, New Orleans, LA, September 1, 2015.

Chapter 5

137. William L. Richter, *Historical Dictionary of the Civil War and Reconstruction* (n.p.: Scarecrow Press, Inc., 2004), 426–27.

138. Ibid., 427.

139. Lee, *St. Bernard Riot*, 16; U.S. Congress, *Testimony Taken by the Committee of Elections, Louisiana*, 104.

140. Lee, *St. Bernard Riot*, 17.

141. Ibid.

142. Ibid., 18.

143. Ibid., 34–35.

144. Ibid., 18.

145. Ibid., 20.

146. Louisiana General Assembly, *Supplemental Report of Joint Committee of the General Assembly of Louisiana on the Conduct of the Late Elections*, xviii.

147. U.S. Congress, *Rooms of Committee on the Conduct of the Late Election and the Condition of Peace and Good Order of the State*, November 27, 1868, 44th Congress, 2nd session, 1868, 253, books.google.com/books?id=pZwFAA AAQAAJ&printsec=frontcover&source=gbs_ge_summary_r&cad=0#v =onepage&q&f=false.

148. Lee, *St. Bernard Riot*, 19.

149. Ibid., 31–32.

150. Ibid., 19–20.

151. Ibid., 20.

152. Ibid., 22.

153. Ibid., 20; U.S. Congress, *Rooms of Committee on the Conduct of the Late Election*, 256.

154. U.S. Congress, *Testimony Taken by the Committee of Elections, Louisiana*, 105.

155. Melinda Meek Hennessey, "Race and Violence in Reconstruction New Orleans: The 1868 Riot," *Louisiana History: The Journal of the Louisiana Historical Association* 20, no. 1 (Winter 1979): 90.

156. Lee, *St. Bernard Riot*, 28.

157. Ibid., 28–29.

158. Ibid., 36.

159. U.S. Congress, *Rooms of Committee on the Conduct of the Late Election* 105, 255.

Chapter 6

160. Lee, *St. Bernard Riot*, 19.

161. U.S. Congress, House of Representatives, *The Miscellaneous Documents*, 1872, 42nd Congress, 2nd session, vol. 4, no. 267, 321, books.google.com/books?id=fC1YAAAAcAAJ&pg=RA1-PA321&lpg#v=onepage&q&f=false.

162. Lee, *St. Bernard Riot*, 25.

163. Ibid., 39.

164. Ibid., 21, 40–42.

165. Ibid., 21.

166. Ibid.

167. Testimony of Phillip Taylor, U.S. Congress, *Rooms of Committee on the Conduct of the Late Election*, 260–61.

168. Rodrigue, *Reconstruction in the Cane Fields*, 101.

169. Ibid., 99–102.

170. Testimony of John Lewis Spalding, *Supplemental Report of Joint Committee of the General Assembly of Louisiana on the Conduct of the Late Elections*, 252.

171. U.S. Congress, *Rooms of Committee on the Conduct of the Late Election*, 254.

172. Ibid.

173. Lee, *St. Bernard Riot*, 43; U.S. Congress, *Rooms of Committee on the Conduct of the Late Election*, 258.

174. Lee, *St. Bernard Riot*, 43.

175. Ibid., 43–44; Louisiana General Assembly, *Supplemental Report of Joint Committee of the General Assembly of Louisiana on the Conduct of the Late Elections*, 263; James Hollandsworth, *An Absolute Massacre: The New Orleans Race Riot of July 30, 1866* (Baton Rouge: Louisiana State University, 2001), 22.

176. U.S. Congress, House of Representatives, *Index to the Executive Documents*, 44th Congress, 2nd Session, 1876–77, 259, books.google.com/books?id=b6AZAAAAYAAJ&pg=PA259&lpg#v=onepage&q&f=false.

177. U.S. Congress, *Rooms of Committee on the Conduct of the Late Election*, 259–60; Lee, *St. Bernard Riot*, 2.

178. Lee, *St. Bernard Riot*, 1, 42.

179. U.S. Congress, *Rooms of Committee on the Conduct of the Late Election*, 253.

180. Ibid., 256–57, 260.

181. Louisiana Congress, *Report of Joint Committee of the General Assembly of Louisiana, On the Conduct of the Late Elections*, 18.

182. U.S. Congress, House of Representatives, *Index to the Executive Documents*, 189.

Chapter 7

183. "U.S. Decennial Census," University of Virginia Library, accessed September 21, 2016, mapserver.lib.virginia.edu.

184. Tennell, *Crucible of Reconstruction*, 156; William Windom and Henry W. Blair, "The Proceedings of a Migration Convention and Congressional Action Respecting the Exodus of 1879," *The Journal of Negro History* 4, no. 1 (January 1919): 51–92, www.jstor.org/stable/2713709.

185. Tennell, *Crucible of Reconstruction*, 156; Hennessey, "Race and Violence in Reconstruction New Orleans," 88.

186. Jerome J. Salomone, *Bread and Respect: The Italians of Louisiana* (Gretna, LA: Pelican Publishing, 2014), 71.

187. Richard Campanella, "Chinatown, New Orleans," *Preservation Resource Center of New Orleans*, November 2013, 16–17.

188. Jung, *Coolies and Cane*, 186–87.

189. Ibid., 204.

190. Tennell, *Crucible of Reconstruction*, 189.

191. Nicholas Lemann, *Redemption: The Last Battle of the Civil War* (New York: Farrar, Straus and Giroux, 2007), 237.

192. Eric Foner, *Reconstruction: America's Unfinished Revolution, 1863–1877* (New York: Perennial Classics, 2002), 550; Rosary O'Neill, *New Orleans Carnival Krewes* (Charleston, SC: The History Press, 2014), 120.

193. Know Louisiana, the Digital Encyclopedia of Louisiana and Home of Louisiana Cultural Vistas, "The Battle of Liberty Place," accessed October 3, 2016, www.knowla.org/entry/757.

194. James K. Hogue, "The 1873 Battle of Colfax: Para-militarism and Counterrevolution in Louisiana," June 2006, 21, warhistorian.org/hogue-colfax.pdf.

195. Rodrigue, *Reconstruction in the Cane Fields*, 176.

196. William Hair, *Bourbonism and Agrarian Protest: Louisiana Politics, 1877–1900* (Baton Rouge: Louisiana State University Press, 1969), 83–90.

197. Ibid., 89–96.

198. Ibid., 83–91.

199. *Daily Picayune*, "Riot in St. Bernard: The Plantation Laborers on Strike," April 19, 1881, 1.

200. *Boston Daily Journal*, "The Labor Movement: A Louisiana Strike," April 20, 1881, 2.

201. *Daily City Item*, "Labor Trouble in St. Bernard," April 20, 1881, 1.

202. *Daily Picayune*, "Murdered in Court," September 16, 1893, 1.

203. Ibid.
204. *New-York Tribune*, "Three Brothers Lynched: Negro Hunting in Louisiana," September 18, 1893, 1.
205. Ibid.
206. *Daily Picayune*, "Execution in St. Bernard: Albert and Charles Goodman Hanged for the Murder of Louis Maspero," November 1, 1884, 8.
207. *New Haven Evening Register*, "A Louisiana Lynching: The Murderer of a Prominent Sugar Planter Is Promptly Dealt With," May 7, 1886, 3.
208. *Daily Item*, "Desperado King: Lynching Party in St. Bernard Parish," December 24, 1894, 1.
209. Ibid.
210. Ibid.
211. *Daily Picayune*, "Midnight Lynching in St. Bernard Parish: James Dandy, the Negro Who Assaulted a White Lady," May 20, 1896, 3; *Birmingham State Herald*, "He'll Dazzle No More: Short Shrift for a Dusky Fiend in St. Bernard Parish, La," May 20, 1896, 1.
212. Din, *Canary Islanders of Louisiana*, 124.
213. Ibid., 124–25; Richard H. Pildes, "Democracy, Anti-Democracy, and the Canon," 2000, 303, accessed November 21, 2015.

Chapter 8

214. Din, *Canary Islanders of Louisiana*, 123; infoweb.newsbank.com.libproxy.tulane.edu:2048/iw-search/we/HistArchive/?p_product=EANX&p_theme=ahnp&p_nbid=X70G5AIRMTQ0MDk4OTU5NS42NTc3NjoxOjEzOjEyOS44MS4yMjYuNzg&p_action=doc&s_lastnonissuequeryname=11&d_viewref=search&p_queryname=11&p_docnum=65&p_docref=v2:1228C1F96EAE924B@EANX-122BB247C0B92E40@2408191-122AC61526BB5FF0@0-123B174F46FAD1C8@.
215. Alcée Fortier, *Louisiana Studies: Literature, Customs and Dialects, History and Education* (New Orleans: F.F. Hansell & Bro., 1894), 199–200.
216. Ibid., 200.
217. Ibid., 200–3.
218. Ibid., 206.
219. Ibid., 207–10.
220. Din, *Canary Islanders of Louisiana*, 128–29.
221. Ibid., 129–30.

222. *Times-Picayune*, "St. Bernard News and Minor Mention: Patrons of Dauphine Line Prepare to Fight Proposed Discontinuance," August 19, 1917, 8B; *New Orleans States*, "Italians to Celebrate," August 10, 1924, 21.

223. Din, *Canary Islanders of Louisiana*, 131.

224. *Daily Picayune*, "In St. Bernard: St. Louis Capitalists, Interested in Reclamation of Lands, Will Visit Parish…," September 9, 1909, 4; *Daily Picayune*, "In St. Bernard: Last St. Bernard Sugar Mill Removed from Parish," August 13, 1910, 4.

225. Din, *Canary Islanders of Louisiana*, 146.

226. Perez, *Isleños of Louisiana*, 51; Din, *Canary Islanders of Louisiana*, 146–49.

227. *Times-Picayune*, "Striking Butchers Nearly All Working: Hence Refuse to Slaughter Cattle Companies Have on Hand," August 28, 1919, 12.

228. *Times-Picayune*, "Butcher's Union Ends Long Strike: Men Back at Work in Rendering and Fertilizing Company," December 20, 1920, 10.

229. *Times-Picayune*, "Sugar Refinery Rioters Shoot Up Employees' Train: One Negro Is Killed and Other Passengers Are Wounded," February 15, 1920, 50; *New Orleans States*, "Motormen Claim Lives in Danger," March 9, 1920, 10; Eric Arnesen, *Waterfront Workers of New Orleans: Race, Class, and Politics, 1863–1923* (Champaign: University of Illinois Press, 1994), 230.

230. Jerry Estopinal (member of the Los Isleños Heritage and Cultural Society), interviewed by C. Dier, St. Bernard, LA, January 22, 2016.

231. Ibid.

232. Peter Pierre (former resident of Fazendeville), interviewed by C. Dier, Meraux, LA, January 22, 2016.

233. Ibid.

234. Ibid.

235. Ibid.

236. Samantha Perez, PhD (Louisiana author and historian), interviewed by C. Dier, New Orleans, LA, May 3, 2017.

237. Maud H. Wallace, "Interview with Ex-Slave Ceceil George in 1940," Louisiana Digital Library, www.louisianadigitallibrary.org/cdm/ref/collection/LWP/id/2698.

INDEX

ABOUT THE AUTHOR

Chris Dier was born in New Orleans and currently teaches history at Chalmette High School in St. Bernard Parish, Louisiana. After Hurricane Katrina, Dier was uprooted to Texas, where he finished high school and attended East Texas Baptist University. Dier received a BA in history from ETBU. After completion of his undergraduate degree, he moved back to his hometown and became an educator to follow in the footsteps of his mother. He continued his studies to earn an MA in education from the University of New Orleans and is currently obtaining a MEd in educational administration from UNO. He resides in St. Bernard Parish and has a keen interest in regional history.

Visit us at
www.historypress.net
....
This title is also available as an e-book